london rooms

ROCKPORT

london

rooms

ROCKPORT PUBLISHERS

Portfolios of
33 Contemporary
Interior Designers
and Architects

Stafford Cliff

First published in the United States of America by
Rockport Publishers, Inc.
33 Commercial Street
Gloucester, Massachusetts 01930-5089
Telephone: (978) 282-9590
Facsimile: (978) 283-2742
www.rockpub.com

ISBN 1-56496-498-1

10 9 8 7 6 5 4 3 2 1

Design: Walter Zekanoski
Front Cover Photograph: Chris Gascoigne
Back Cover Photographs: (from top) Chris Gascoigne, James Morris/Axiom
and Henry Wilson/The Interior Archive

Printed in China.

Dedicated to John Scott, with my unlimited gratitude for his constant assistance, enthusiasm, and support.

ACKNOWLEDGMENTS

My thanks to all those talented architects and designers for responding so enthusiastically to my calls and for providing photographs and information, and my apologies to those who could not be included or whose latest project was not finished in time to go to press. Thanks also to the photographers who helped by documenting these London Rooms with such style. Their names appear on page 192.

In addition, I am indebted to Yvonne Jordan at View Pictures, Lucy Waitt at Arcaid, and Karen Howes at the Interior Archive. To Eric Morin, Ian Hogarth, Diana Salevourakis, Flora Fairbairn, and Seth Stein. Most importantly, thanks to project manager Francine Hornberger, art director Stephen Perfetto, and editor and inspiration Martha Wetherill.

CONTENTS

INTRODUCTION

IF YOU COULD buzz around in a little helicopter and visit every architect and interior designer working on contemporary residential projects in London today—zooming in on their drawing boards, downloading their computers, examining their architectural models, and following them onto building sites—what you might find is what appears in this book. *London Rooms* showcases what tourists never see. And because most of this work has been done for private clients, many of the pictures were taken only for the designers' portfolios and won't ever appear in magazines.

When the material was collected for this book, each consultant was asked to choose his or her latest or most imaginative recent project, one that they thought best represented the work they're doing today and intend to continue with in the future. In almost every case, they nominated their very latest jobs, sometimes commissioning special photography or waiting for the finishing touches to go in or the furniture to arrive. In several houses, the new owners had agreed to abandon all their existing furniture and start again with a clean slate, with pieces commissioned from or chosen by the designers to complement the scheme.

Monitoring the trends in domestic architecture is perhaps a bit like following our nightly weather forecast for London and the Southeast: High pressure coming in, bringing with it across the Atlantic more industrial conversions and loft-style developments, accompanied by ever-increasing imagination in rejuvenating traditional townhouses and Victorian villas. The loft concept came from the U.S., but it has been reinterpreted by British architects and designers to create a style unique to the U.K.

In London, we're in the midst of a major trend of people wanting to move back into the cities—to spend more time with their families; with personal projects; to walk to work; and, as one designer put it, "to do some nest building." In contrast to the 1920s, when people were encouraged to move to the suburbs, or the 1960s when the trend was to find "a little place in the country," Londoners today are happy to enjoy more urban surroundings, to convert and reenergize commercial spaces, even to rediscover onetime unpopular high-rise apartment buildings or neglected inner boroughs. Suddenly, it's not only fashionable to live five minutes from work, it's in demand. On top of that, people want to be near the best restaurants and shops—to enjoy street markets, lively cafes, late-night shopping, cross-cultural events, and Sunday mornings in the park.

In urban settings, however, planning restrictions might apply, space is sometimes limited, or, in some cases, prior industrial spaces are called upon to become homes. Each situation presents its own new challenges for the design professional. Architects have responded with imaginative and ambitious solutions for transforming even the most unpromising "shoe boxes." The tiniest urban living spaces need to look good, to have good natural light, practical planning, economical heating, and lots of storage space.

At a time when we are used to staying in designer hotels, eating in designer restaurants, and shopping in environments created by the world's best interior designers and architects, there is now a trend to commission that same designer for our abodes. *London Rooms* shows how this desire is affecting the way we would like to live at home.

RICK
MATHER

THIS SEEMINGLY solid concrete box with its open terraces and unusual window placement turns out to be a light-filled structure of glass and pale wood, transparent stairs and roofs, brides and balconies—all hovering above a ground-floor swimming pool.

Rick Mather's considerable experience spans both private and public buildings—including restaurants, theaters, museums, and colleges, and his skill at creating large-scale master planning for world heritage sites is balanced by his sensitivity to smaller structures that sit happily in their environment, whether it be a Georgian terrace or a 1960s East Anglican University. So when asked by the owners of this private house in Hampstead, North London, to submit a proposal, it was his sympathy for the site and his strategy for dealing with sensitive residential considerations that got him the job. He even staged a small exhibition of the new proposals for the neighbors, the local conservation societies, and council members to win their support before work began.

The client wanted a house with roof gardens, a swimming pool, and an abundance of natural light on a steeply sloping site, and Mather and his team, led by senior associate Douglas McIntosh, responded by creating this imaginative solution. The concrete frame supports large voids and cantilevered floors over the pool, and structural glass is used extensively throughout the house including skylights, glass floors (which provide light deep into the plan), glass stairs and balustrading, and external floorlights, which allow light from the basement to illuminate the front facade. The owners liken it to living inside a huge sculpture full of unexpected views and a variety of different spaces, and even the neighbors say they are pleased with the results.

ABOVE AND OPPOSITE Two views of the soaring internal space with its shapes and patterns made as much by the light as by the combination of columns, terraces, walkways, and balustrades, some solid and some transparent—in ½-inch (15 mm) tempered glass. Calm is achieved by the lining up of these planes, and the lack of fussy detailing, though the rooms are full of interesting touches, like the tiny window (THIS PAGE) that allows a view from the master bedroom into the stair void.

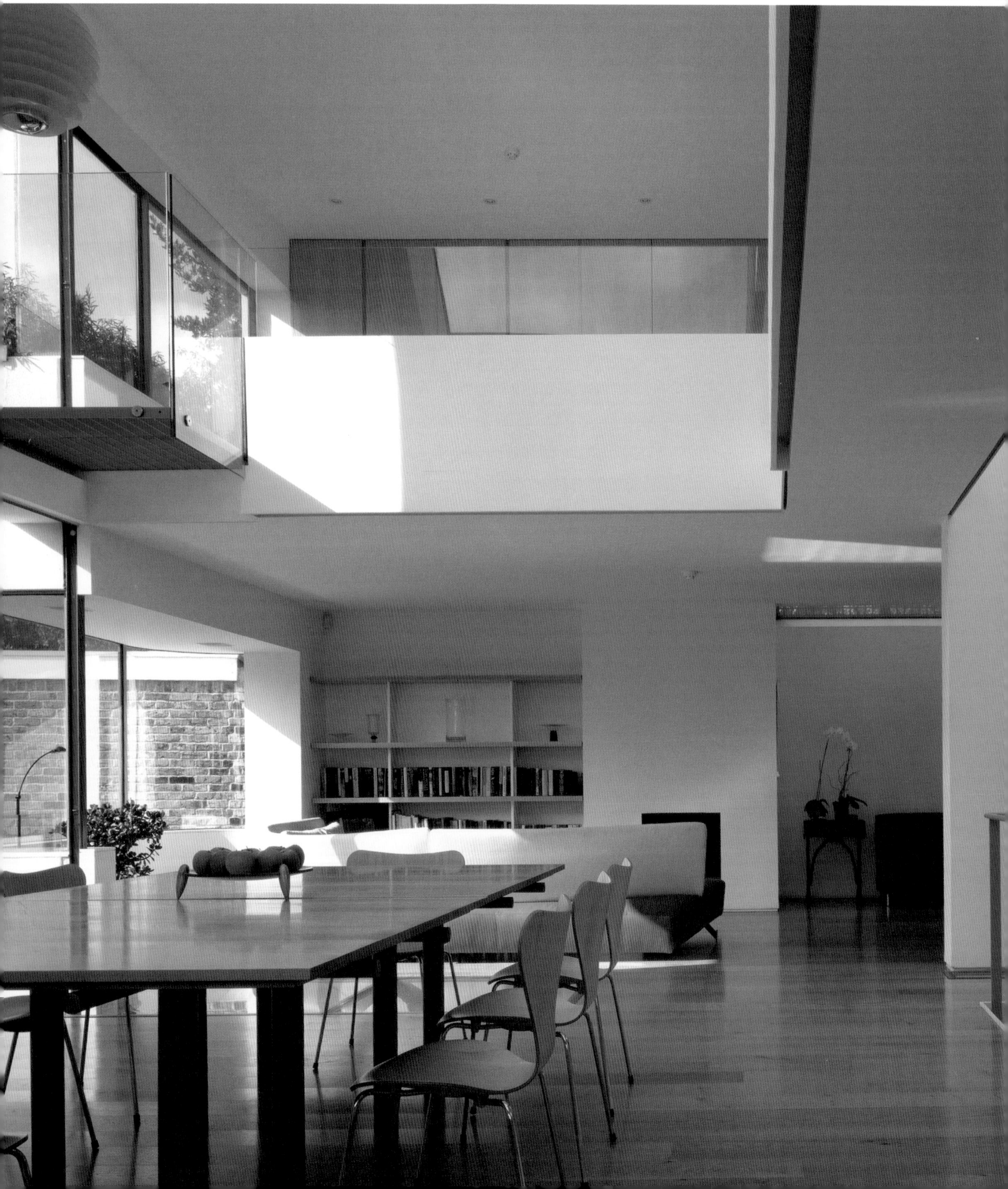

ABOVE Above the pool, laminated glass stairs with an acid-etched pattern to give grip and highlight the nozings—lead to the rooms above without blocking any light and the line of an overhead bridge matches a large window that opens onto a garden room that doubles as a guest room.

LEFT Large family gatherings take place on the main floor of the house. Stairs continue up to a walkway that leads to a small gallery where floor-to-ceiling cupboards conceal his-and-her work areas. When the cupboards are open, the gallery becomes a study. A small viewing platform, like a glass box, is cantilevered partly inside, partly outside the house.

STANTON
WILLIAMS

ON THE ROOF of a recently refurbished factory building in North London, Stanton Williams created not only a spare and spacious combination of living and working functions, but a kaleidoscope of light. "We're passionate model makers here," says partner Paul Williams, explaining how they studied the path of the sun, where it rises and sets, and how it falls on the building at different times of the day and in different seasons. Most particularly, they know about the different colors of light—warmer and cooler—at different times of the day, and how to used bounced light and shadows to help model the spaces like a painter would. It might have helped that their client, a graphic designer, was also visually driven, and keen on the purity of space.

To a certain extent, the shape of the structure was defined by the roof and the position of the lift from below, but the client wanted the space to be designed in a way that allowed the main open-plan central living area to double as a place for client meetings without it feeling overtly domestic. At the same time, Stanton Williams devised screens and sliding panels so that if she wished, the client could open out the whole apartment and see right through. Most importantly, the architects' plan was to conceive the inside and the outside as one space, dissolving the barrier between the two, and—by the use of similar materials and overlapping levels— make the external space internal, and the apartment seem twice the size.

THIS PAGE Throughout the apartment, the floor is ¼-inch- (6 mm) thick, pale sycamore lamination to plywood panels. Large, semiopaque white blinds, can be lowered to screen the windows and the view over London suburbs.

OPPOSITE At one end of the apartment, the raised level of the terrace is drawn through the glass to define a third bedroom area that can be closed off by a sycamore screen.

FOLLOWING PAGE While making maximum use of light and shade during the day, at night, the rooftop space gets most impact from its graphic simplicity and rationalized range of colors and materials.

Looking toward the designer's studio, the slender columns are placed away from the line of glazing, which has been trained with stainless steel, and a louvered canopy diffuses the light outside.

MARK GUARD

TOO MANY FUNCTIONS and not enough space. That was the problem faced by architect Mark Guard and his team in this relatively low-ceilinged industrial conversion just a few yards from the Thames. As well as wanting to maximize the living area, the client also wanted to include two bedrooms and two bathrooms. The solution was to combine the sleeping platforms with another function.

The master bed sits above a dressing area, accessed through a large pivoting door. The guest bed, adjacent to the main entrance, is sited atop a guest bathroom. The circular stainless steel shower extends into the main living area and provides a sculptural counterpart to the more geometric forms of the master bed. A stone-clad hit-or-miss staircase provides the route up to the guest sleeping platform.

A concrete pillar, part of the building's original structure, has been left untouched in the main living area. The kitchen is set behind a freestanding counter with a tempered glass storage shelf. This counter contains the oven, stovetop, preparation surfaces, and waste. All surfaces within the apartment are finished in white with smooth, flush-fitting doors and cupboards.

OPPOSITE Steps on the right lead up to the master bedroom. Beyond this is the circular enclosure that houses the bathroom, up four steps at the end. The whole area can be screened off by the large sliding canvas screen.

BELOW The floor in the master bathroom is electrically heated Piedra Plano, or Portuguese limestone. The mirror above the stainless steel washbasin conceals a small cabinet, and the rungs lead directly to the bed platform above.

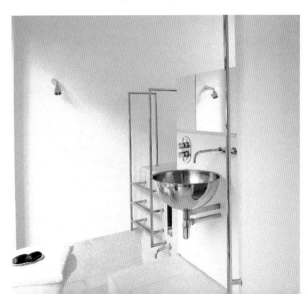

LEFT A recess in the ceiling gives extra headroom to the second bedroom—once guests have negotiated what the architect calls a "hit-or-miss" staircase of staggered limestone columns.

OPPOSITE As a reminder of the apartment's previous life, one column was left in its raw concrete state, contrasting with the all-white surfaces elsewhere.

FOLLOWING PAGES Cooking, eating, and relaxing all share the main space of this apartment, and because the oven and stove are placed in the central unit, the cook can face into the room. The sink can be hidden by flush-fitting doors. The freestanding oval stainless steel drum is a small breakfast table with two roll-out chairs.

WELLS MACKERETH

AN EXISTING MEZZANINE was torn out to take maximum advantage of the full volume in this two-bedroom 174-square-yard (145 m²) apartment. Wells Mackereth wanted the space to feel as airy as possible for a client who works from home. All the storage units were designed to be taller than the average head height, and a lightweight ladder can be attached to a perimeter rail to gain access to cupboards and storage platforms on the wall that divides the living and sleeping spaces. Along the wall at the far end, the fitted kitchen establishes a feeling of generosity, with tall stainless steel and medium-density fiberboard cabinetry. The table, with a black walnut-veneered top, was also designed to expand in length. Elsewhere, the apartment is full of ingenious detailing—sliding doors, push-and-tilt panels, lightweight shutters, and pivoting full-height doors.

OPPOSITE A tall dividing wall stops short of the width and conceals high-level storage, a sliding shuttered desk, and **(TO THE LEFT)** a fireplace. The door on the right leads to the entrance lobby.

BELOW The linear feeling in this scheme is continued in the furnishing with the extendible table and unit seating all placed square-on to the enormous windows. The ceiling beams, too damaged to be left untreated, were sprayed with a faux-concrete finish.

ABOVE One end of the space is devoted to the master bedroom with a bathroom cantilevered at high level into the room, and a second bathroom and a walk-in dressing room, behind sliding doors below.

OPPOSITE Looking toward the bedrooms, the narrow corridor can be closed off by a full-height, wired-glass, pivoting panel.

ABOVE AND OPPOSITE From the main bedroom, a floating stair leads to the mezzanine bathroom, where the sunken bath is set in cumbrian slate dais that also embraces a long bench in American black walnut.

MMM
ARCHITECTS

THIS APARTMENT doesn't look like a typical loft space, and that's just what the client wanted. Though loft living in London is now enormously popular, many architects are looking for new ways to treat the once-commercial spaces, and clients are becoming more conversant with architectural styles and building materials. The client asked MMM Architects for something simple and rugged in both space design and finish—without being self-conscious or contrived. In the tall, narrow top-floor space, the architects created a solution that respected the character of the original warehouse building—retaining the old wooden floorboards (newly sanded and sealed), restoring the brickwork, and introducing a steel staircase. In contrast, to articulate the "working" zone, the kitchen/ dining area/bathroom, was placed on a raised limestone deck that appears to float by touching neither the walls nor the staircase. In this way, the concept of minimal intervention— the feeling that these things could all one day be removed, and the character of the old building be restored—is maintained.

OPPOSITE The original floorboards in the living room are complemented by a wall paneled in rippled sycamore and a steel roof beam that reveals part of the original structure of the building. Set into the windows is a full-height Iroko framed glass door that leads to a balcony, and camber-style louvers that allow air to circulate.

BELOW In the central core of the space, a freestanding steel staircase was introduced to link the upper terrace and appear as a leftover from the original building.

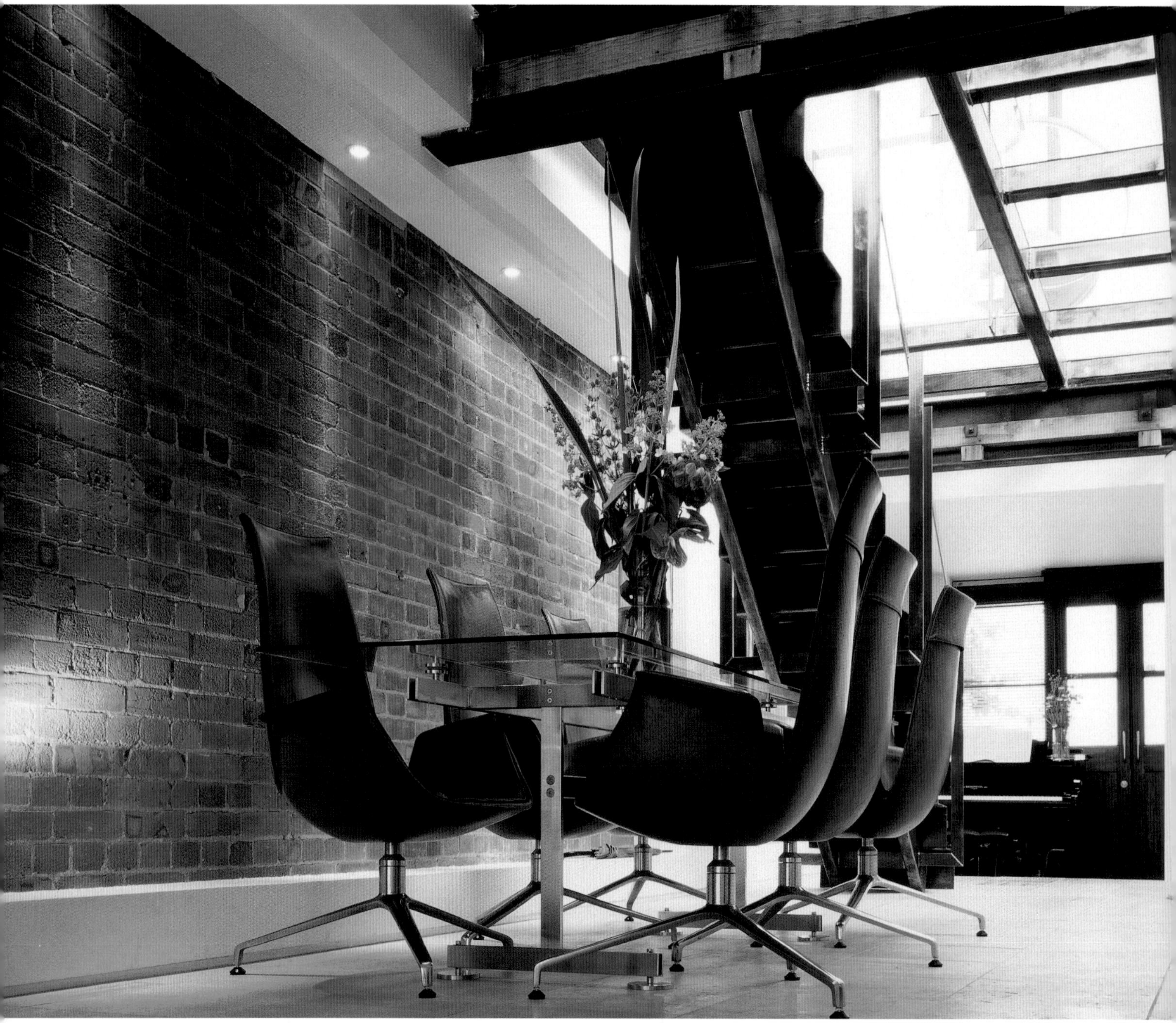

ABOVE AND LEFT The central service block is balanced above by a lighter-weight glass floor in the lantern void that, with its metal framing, continues the "new against old, heavy against light" philosophy of the scheme. In the kitchen, the floor-to-ceiling cupboards are sycamore, and the work surface on the projecting countertop is Welsh mountain slate.

FOLLOWING PAGES Framed and lit like a piece of artwork, the original brickwork was sandblasted and sealed to keep out the dust. On the right, a glass door leads into the bathroom.

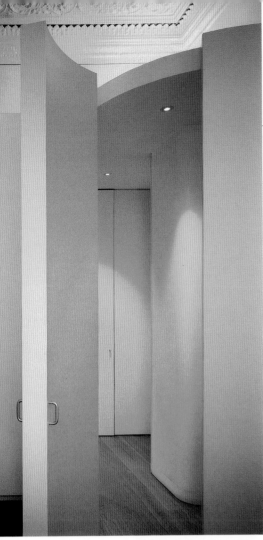

WILL
WHITE

HAVING PREVIOUSLY LIVED in a five-story house with "too many small-scale rooms connected by endless stairs," the client wanted to change her living space from a house to an apartment: to have horizontal space as opposed to vertical orientation; the ability to hang larger-scale art works within a living environment for personal pleasure and with the possibility of mounting occasional shows within the apartment; and the ability to close up the apartment when traveling aboard.

Immediately seizing on the potential of the grade II listed building in a garden square in Baywater, West London, previously divided into series of studio apartments with no kitchen, bathroom or services, White stripped out all the subdivisions and makeshift sleeping platforms, and set about reinstating the principal first-floor reception rooms as a single space with original features. To this, he added a kitchen and dining area big enough for entertaining, a main bedroom with en-suite dressing and shower room, a guest bedroom with cloakroom and bath, and plenty of storage.

To complicate matters, the space actually spanned two adjoining buildings on slightly different levels—what the architect calls a "lateral conversion"—so while maintaining the large rooms with their beautiful 9-foot- (2.7 m) high doors, White also had to provide access and circulation.

LEFT, OPPOSITE, AND PAGE 40 The simplicity of the scheme can be summarized by this series of doorway glimpses: original doorways with architrave still in place **(FAR LEFT)** are contrasted with new apertures, some flush to the wall **(LEFT)**, some as a freestanding curved intrusion **(ABOVE LEFT)**. To add drama in the almost entirely white apartment, the architect used a single color (yellow) on the inside of the curved lobby in the hallway, and in the interiors of all the cupboards.

FOLLOWING PAGES Although extensive structural work was done, this room now seems so calm that the eye is focused only on the individual pieces, a combination of the client's original furniture, with some larger-scale new additions. The antique marble fireplace was added to reflect the spirit of the original building, as was the 7-inch- (175 mm) wide, extra-long American oak floorboards.

ABOVE Using the same spirit and the same all-white walls and window shades, the kitchen was positioned on the same first floor level, but in what was once the building next door. White treated the units as a freestanding piece of furniture, and adapting Bulthaup System 25, he created one level with all metal walls and countertops and roller shutters instead of cabinet doors, and the other level, an island unit, in lacquered doors and a honed granite countertop.

ABOVE To allow daylight to enter the downstairs bathroom Will White replaced a door with a frosted, glazed panel of glass.

MOUTARDE

THE BIGGEST CHALLENGE facing architects who set out to convert industrial spaces and make them more practical for domestic use is the problem of how to divide them up. Where once artists and designers were happy to scatter a few key pieces of furniture artistically around a vast open space, now people want to live in more domestic proportions, with zones for public and private use. This solution then, must surely be one of the most original.

The top floor of an old concrete-and-brick paint factory in Shoreditch, East London, was being sold as a shell when interior designer Heidi Wish acquired it. Her old apartment had two bedrooms and two bathrooms in a space of 700 square feet (65 m²). Now, she was faced with 2,200 square feet (205 m²). She didn't want one big space, but she also knew she didn't want to carve it up into little boxes. She wanted a big bedroom and bathroom (with a window), plenty of work surface in the kitchen, lots of storage space, and to be able to expand the work area or build another bedroom and bathroom at a later stage. In addition, she wanted it to be practical and functional.

After looking at various planning options, Moutarde started marking out the spaces in chalk on the floor, but the solution didn't really come together until, at an art gallery, they saw an installation that included a copper-lined box that gave you a feeling of dimesionlessness when you looked into it. They couldn't achieve that effect, but it gave them the inspiration they were looking for—a means of dividing the loft into private and public—cooking and eating separated from sleeping, bathing, and working, via a concrete-style tunnel and a wall of fiery red glass.

LEFT Like a glowing reflective artwork, the glass wall conceals the bath and shower to the left and a storage area to the right. Though Wish found a lot of pieces in markets and scrap yards, this sofa—a new design—is by her friend Andrew Stafford.

ABOVE Slicing like a seemingly endless concrete tunnel through a wall of glass, the corridor that links the living and sleeping/working spaces of the loft was constructed in rendered block work. The glass was made by laminated glass specialist Sean Butler, and the poured concrete floor concealed the heating. Various pieces of furniture were designed and made by friends, including this table by Richard Dewhurst.

OPPOSITE To allow for plumbing and services, the bathroom (BACK RIGHT) was built on a raised platform. The fixtures came from a second-hand shop. The bed is set into a raised cherry-veneered platform.

IN THIS RADICAL REDESIGN of a three-story house in the Notting Hill district, a sequence of small and inadequately sized rooms was removed, new floors created, and a rear extension added. In fact, only the front facade was retained.

In the new design, the entry level became the focus of the house: the kitchen was relocated here, together with the dining area. The living room was moved to the top (first) floor, up toward the light, and became one simple open room occupying the whole of the first floor. The bedrooms were relocated from the first floor to the lower ground floor, where a sequence of recesses and storage areas created the sleeping and dressing areas, with the master bathroom off the sleeping area, in the rear extension.

The substantial remodeling gave an opportunity to rethink the way in which one moved from floor to floor through the house. There was also a desire to add some spatial drama to the house, to open up and link the three levels vertically. The old dog-leg staircases were stripped out and a vertical space was created along the party wall on one side, on the axis of the entrance from the street, and top-lit by a new skylight that runs continuously from front to back. This skylight brings light down into the middle of the house.

In order to make the linked idea of skylight and new vertical space work, an idea that seeks to counterbalance the typical stacked horizontality of the London terraced house, a staircase of lightness and transparency was required at ground floor to mediate the three levels. The solution was innovative laminated-glass treads using structural silicone and a newly developed transparent structural tape. And because the house was so small, the architects minimized the elements within the staircase, creating a sheer glass wall on one side and supporting the treads on the other side, on a steel "flat" built into the finish of the party wall. The result is a feeling of lightness and transparency, where a conventional stair would have obstructed both.

ABOVE A sheer glass wall, divided into three separate sections to allow it to be brought into the house, serves as the structural support for one side of the staircase, as well as provides the balustrade for the staircase itself and also for the first floor.

OPPOSITE In contrast, a beech floor was used for the whole first floor to provide warmth for a room that was designed for reflection and repose. The tiny London townhouse gives no hint of the radical makeover it received inside, apart from the delicate green paint, which previews the innovative glass stair just inside the front door.

RIGHT AND OPPOSITE The stairs' only metal components are the special stainless "shoes" designed to bear the laminated treads and glass floors and the disk-shaped mechanical braces that hold the vertical laminated glass sheets to the floor structure.

IT HAS BEEN SAID that Adjaye and Russell display a fresh post-Recession energy that is currently bringing new life to British architecture. Their skill at creating a flexible environment is what drew the owners of this space—a refurbished 1930s office building in Clerkenwell—to them. The 15,000-square-foot (1395 m²) shell on the fourth floor was a long rectangular unit with very large windows at either end, which the clients wanted to keep. In fact it was "their little dream," as David Adjaye puts it, to have an apartment with no walls and a new way of living. They even abandoned all their existing furniture and possessions, apart, that is, from a huge collection of memorabilia that had to be provided for. "It was a bland space—perfect for us to take our ideas of transparency and mobility to their conclusion—push it as far as it could go," explains Adjaye.

Since they set up business in 1994, David Adjaye and William Russell's work has included homes for high-profile clients including Ewan McGregor, Wolfgang Joop, and Alexander McQueen. Adjaye attributes their success to an unconventional use of industrial materials in the home environment. "We like the way, that in a domestic context, they become something different," he has said.

PREVIOUS PAGES Though they had a sense of what it would be like, the owners couldn't picture it, so Adjaye and Russell created a model to illustrate the various ways the space could be changed. Mostly in black and grays, all the interventions are either dark or luminous, some with the sheen of a grand piano. This view, toward the sleeping area, has the kitchen with its sliding screens partially concealed on the right.

ABOVE AND RIGHT Floor-to-ceiling pivoting screens covered in natural felt separate the bedroom and bathroom end. The bed folds away behind flush-fitting doors and the bathtub—treated as a piece of furniture— has a lid that slides across to close it off. Throughout the space, the floor was raised to install heating and then a slatelike finish of poured composite resin, more often seen in sports buildings, was applied. The storage wall along one side of the apartment ("the working part") is all bespoke joinery lacquered dark green. The library has two layers of shelves, one of which rolls out to reveal the second and breaks up the space.

OPPOSITE To accommodate the owners' collection, Adjaye and Russell created a raised platform with individually illuminated divisions, each covered by a panel of reinforced glass with etched strips to prevent slipping.

ABOVE A corridor behind the bed leads from the sink to the shower. The lift-up chests are for sweaters and all the woodwork is in Douglas fir.

KELLY HOPPEN

WORKING IN A STYLE she calls East-West, Kelly Hoppen has created some of the most stylish, most photographed London interiors in the past five years and her style is fast becoming as well-known abroad. She has said of her interiors that they look at first glance—with their collections of artworks and artifacts—that they could belong to an art collector or an explorer. "Yet there is a tranquillity, and a love of clear color and subtle texture, that can only be of today," she says, "a distillation of influences from both East and West." Certainly that seems true of this penthouse apartment in central London.

The initial brief was to make the place a sanctuary in neutral colors, but Hoppen has also made it a place of fantasy, in which to escape the harshness of the outside world. An interior should, she thinks, "be flexible enough to be changed according to mood." Without making any structural changes, the designer was let loose to completely furnish the two-level residence, down to the very last detail. She even organized the housewarming party—which was the first time the client actually saw the completed scheme.

OPPOSITE Living room, looking into the dining room, displaying accoutrements demonstrating Hoppen's classic "distillation of influences from both East and West."

LEFT Flowers are always an integral part of Hoppen's schemes—often matching in color, arranged in sculptural shapes, or evoking exotic origins.

RIGHT Adding texture rather than pattern, the windows along one wall in the living room can be covered by a sheer fabric whose track is concealed in a recess created by the ceiling moulding.

OPPOSITE Floor-to-ceiling sliding screens, covered in faux suede fabric to match the loose covers on the dining room chairs, separate the dining room from the central hallway that leads to the kitchen.

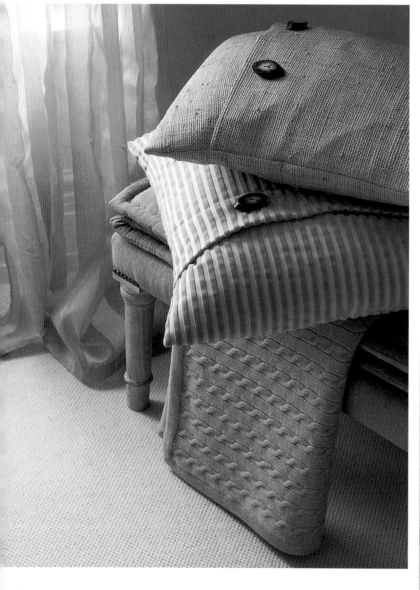

ABOVE "Texture is the new color," says Kelly Hoppen, referring to her use of fabrics on cushions, throws, and drapes.

OPPOSITE In the master bedroom, the moleskin bedcover sports two wide bands—another Hoppen trademark.

RUFFLE
& HOOK

CAROL THOMAS OF RUFFLE & HOOK has a rebellious approach to color and texture. She wants every color to zing, fabrics to be soft and "yummy," and paint to be as hard as nail polish. To test her skills, she recently decorated a spectacular old converted bank building in East London. The building had already been converted and "modernized" in the 1960s, with new floors put in and some of the Neoclassical features unfortunately removed. Thomas's idea was to base the interior on a grand Italian palazzo, with multiple living rooms downstairs, a music room/library above, and smaller bedrooms, bathrooms, and studies on the second and third floors. But the designer's nature did not require her to stick rigidly to the concept. She mixed concrete and medium-density fiberboard with fine antiques; architectural salvage with upholstered tailoring; and inexpensive hessian with velvets and voiles. In fact, her two curtain-making shops are well known for their unexpected and surprising combinations of materials— and her sense of fun infuses everything she does.

RIGHT At street level, the long wall has its original windows but the designer has used linoleum instead of marble on the floor and installed oversized 14-foot- (4.3 m) high doors to give a theatrical entrance to the kitchen.

LEFT In the sitting room, the provincial-size fireplace that gives the room its focus was made from concrete. The walls are given extra depth by the application of four layers of emulsion paint.

OPPOSITE In one of the small upstairs bedrooms, Carol Thomas washed the rafters with white stain and combined various antiques and junk-shop finds, including an American mirror.

ABOVE Elegant shapes and pale colors come into play when simplicity and understatement are needed. The brilliant sides of this tub and matching roller blind tassels create the zing.

CARDEN
CUNIETTI

IT'S DIFFICULT TO IMAGINE, but this first-floor flat in West London was originally divided into several small rooms. The fact that it now looks bright and spacious is thanks to the owner and partner Audrey Carden of Carden Cunietti— who promptly knocked down all the walls and turned it into one large living area with a bathroom and one bedroom. A mezzanine level was installed above a small kitchen in one corner, and the whole apartment was furnished with a combination of contemporary and 1940s pieces—bold shapes and strong colors against bright white walls—a solution that embodies the design team's signature style.

RIGHT AND BELOW In the huge living room, the old floorboards were stained and varnished and two French windows give access to a typical London portico terrace. The French daybed is covered in red cotton, and forms a divide between the sitting and dining areas. In one corner, a large glazed ceramic pot stands on a small cabinet beside a French 1940s lamp with a raffia-bound shade on a wood and animal-skin African drum. The only pattern comes from the 1930s horsehair car blanket covering the seat of a bent-wood chair that came from a flea market.

ABOVE A Victorian cast iron spiral stair with carved wood handrail leads to a small mezzanine, and was reclaimed from another project. The dining table and chairs are original 1940s pieces, and the cabinet is a Carden Cunietti design.

TOP Through still part of the room, the mezzanine has a glass balustrade and is used as a more private space for watching TV or listening to music.

BOTTOM In the bedroom, the furniture is inspired by 1940s designs and the cabinetry uses a classic design with the addition of bamboo inserts to give it a warm exotic feeling that also echoes the grain of the woodwork.

THOUGH THE FEELING in this penthouse apartment is that of a finely crafted boat, with all the woodwork and much of the cabinetry designed by Simon Foxell at The Architects Practice, the starting point for the interior was color. The the color scheme—which changes from space to space in the open-plan apartment, to the rugs and soft furnishings—consists of rich Chinese red, cinnamon, and burnt orange. Natural materials, such as oak and cherry woods, copper, ceramic, glass, limestone, and leather, help to create a warm tactile combination with the colors in the specially designed and manufactured rugs by Helen Yardley. At the center of the apartment is the most spectacular piece: a vast chandelier hanging in a shallow dome in the ceiling of the living area, which is hung with thousands of overlapping handmade ceramic tiles.

RIGHT A view across the width of the apartment shows the fitness area, with its oak wallbars. On the loft, a small bar has been set into an alcove in the billards room, where the pool table doubles as a surface for extra-large dinner parties.

OPPOSITE Though most of the structure of this conservatory-style space over-looking Kensington Gardens was already in place, the architects introduced electronically adjustable external louvers to the skylights.

FOLLOWING PAGES The rear elevation seems almost to blend into the garden with overhead glazing and huge doors and decking to bridge the transition.

ASH
SAKULA

THOUGH THERE ARE STILL ROOMS in this building that await renovation and their full quota of proper furniture, the real heart of the house is this one space with its overlapping functions.

When the architects first saw this house in a suburban neighborhood, it was oddly dark and silent with many rooms, many books on Christian philosophy and religion, and a huge collection of deer, elk, and fox heads emerging from any available wall space. The new owners wanted a cheerful house with lots of space. Ash Sakula accomplished this by adding many steel beams and a couple of columns, as well as opening the back of the house to its garden and constructing a large deck that extends the living space still further and acts as an intermediary level to the much lower lawn.

The glass-roofed extensions bring the height and drama of a nearby eucalyptus and more distant laburnum tree with their distinct shapes and contrasting colors, deep into the house.

The working area of the kitchen was conceived as a series of objects. Cupboards and countertops form satellites around the relatively tight core of the essential appliances. Each object has its own shape, color, composition, and, together, form a kind of interior landscape, one the architects wanted to "still look good after a party-under stacks of dirty dishes; one that made for interesting contemplation during a boring dinner party."

RIGHT The children's sunken play area is the media room where the adults hang out after hours watching others cook and catching the TV news (television, VCR, and stereo are housed behind the refrigerator).

OPPOSITE The architects planed this ground-floor space as a landscape gardener would when considering the impact that different plants will have through the seasons and over time. They wanted the colors and shapes they were making to form a robust framework for the changing cast of bottles, pans, plates, and glasses as they came and went.

OPPOSITE The top floor had its red tile roof cut with a builder's scalpel to throw light down the deep stairwell, leading the eye through a light-filled passage across the floor of a new studio to the trees on the horizon.

ABOVE LEFT The adults have another play area, under the glass roof, in which to read papers and listen to music. The space also functions as the hard bright space where the children can draw or run car races on a gloomy winter's day.

ABOVE RIGHT The shower room was a response to the clients' need to shower simultaneously. Combining two side-by-side mosaic and concrete alcoves along one wall, the plan of the room relies on a combination of curves and floating panels. Storage is concealed behind walls and mirrors combine with chrome and slate around the sink, which is balanced on the right by a lower slate bench.

PERHAPS IN LONDON more than anywhere else, when a designer and client meet to talk about a brief for a new scheme, at some point the conversation inevitably centers around the quality of light. Though this interior is dramatically different from most peoples' idea of home, in regard to lighting, it was no exception. A concrete "shell" in an old industrial building in East London, the huge space had big windows on either side. The client—a photographer —wanted to keep the space open and maintain both sources of light.

It was the first domestic job 24/Seven had done and they were keen to apply the expertise they had gained designing exhibitions and workspaces in the Capital. At the same time, they wanted to let the space dictate the design, rather than impose a scheme or their own view—they even had to step in when the contractor got carried away and began to repaint over the peeling walls. The designers' key concept was "utilitarian." They kept everything simple, stripped-down, and open, introducing pressed steel, concrete, and white brick tiles like those used on London's underground—with a rough French oak floor supplementing the existing concrete. Most radically, to add additional drama and to provide an entrance lobby and storage spaces, they punctured the room from side to side with a long angled wall of pressed-steel floor plates left over from a previous job.

ABOVE Set against the area of white glazed tiles in the bathroom is an old fashioned Belfast sink, once only used in washhouses, and Markwick hospital style mixer taps.

RIGHT To define the bathroom space, 24/Seven set the shower, sink, and salvaged bathtub on a concrete platform that provided space below for plumbing. One part of the wall was tiled to match the existing glazed-brick columns and one wall left as peeling paintwork.

PREVIOUS PAGES Leaving the long concrete shell as open as possible, 24/Seven kept all the materials in the same utilitarian vein, adding a new oak floor that emphasizes the width by running crossways, and surface-fixed wiring to floodlight the ceiling. At one end, the designers placed the bed and work area, and at the other, the kitchen and living area.

PATEL
TAYLOR

APART FROM ONE monolithic site-formed concrete wall, everything in this loft apartment seems to be floating. Walls and ceilings hover without touching, light contrasts with dark, and rough meets smooth. Old materials abut new ones and New York meets Japan. What at first seems simple is, in fact, extremely complicated and finely detailed, with every vista revealing (or concealing) new planes, and every surface joined in a sensitive way. Not even the door handles—made of leather thongs—are a traditional solution.

The starting point for Pankaj Patel at Patel Taylor Architects, was an impressive 3,500-square-foot (326 m²), 16-foot- (5 m) high empty shell in a two-story Victorian tobacco warehouse in Battersea. The client wanted a combination of private accommodation, including three bedrooms and three bathrooms, without destroying the unique volume of the space. At the same time, she wanted to take better advantage of the view from one window—of the adjacent dock. One side of the loft was left as open as possible, allowing natural light in from three sides, while the other incorporates the more closed areas. But one of the key challenges, according to the architects, was how to manipulate the scale of all these components, and make them all work in one overall scheme.

RIGHT To the left of the entrance, a corridor, echoed by the ceiling, which was cut away to allow the top of the warehouse's original iron column to show, links the bedrooms and bathrooms.

OPPOSITE The construction sequence was determined by the erection on site of the solid concrete wall. Changes in floor finish were designed to indicate the different uses of the space, and the timber slatted ceiling panels were floated 15½ inches (400 mm) off the gray-painted concrete, allowing space above for an acoustic quilt.

FOLLOWING PAGES The external wall line on one side has been brought inside the main envelope in the form of a full-height minimal glass screen, allowing the creation of a Venetian-inspired loggia space and a wide curved balcony from which to view the boats outside. All the furniture and fabrics were chosen by Tara Bernerd to complement the space.

OPPOSITE To the left of the entrance, a corridor, echoed by the ceiling, which was cut away to allow the top of the warehouse's original iron column to show, links the bedrooms and bathrooms.

ABOVE The largest central space in the interior is occupied only by two colonial teak and rattan daybeds. The living, dining, and kitchen spaces flow into each other, defined only by the insertion of floating ceilings, screens, shutters, ledges, and flooring changes.

JONATHAN REED

MOST OF THE WORK done by Jonathan Reed's company, Reed Creative Services, involves interior architecture and restructuring. But when it came to his own apartment—a 2,000-square-foot (186 m²) unit in Chelsea, he was restricted by a local preservation order from making any changes to the building. The space—an entire floor of a 1890s building on King's Road that was once used as a town hall—is unusual for this area, where most people live in multiple-room apartments in purpose-built mansion blocks or small terraced houses. Reed has responded by dividing the space in halves with a low screen, and creating zones of furniture—grouping classic pieces from his collection of twentieth-century furniture with new prototypes by his own studio. The result is a testimony to his skill in using disparate components, his eye for shape and color, and his love of rich surfaces and textures.

OPPOSITE Unable to move any walls or add any ceiling lights, Reed painted the whole space white and relied on a collection of lamps, including one by Carlo Mollino and one made from string. The floor is set in an oak border and the curtains are unlined wall felt, pierced by aluminum poles. A 1970s sofa by Paul McCobb is set near a pair of 1940s Danish chairs.

BELOW An ottoman that doubles as a coffee table by the addition of a fragment of Welsh slate.

ABOVE A low screen made by Reed from American black walnut and hinged with carpet binding tape helps to divide the living area behind two 1960s Finnish leather chairs and a leather-covered drum table. The lamp, a post-war British design, is by John and Sylvia Reid.

OPPOSITE In front of a working fireplace with a black slate surround, the two-level kitchen houses an oven and stove below a black Corian work surface.

PREVIOUS PAGES The designer's own treasures are seen in this corner of the apartment: a large Aring surplus metal closet (on new oak legs), which forms a backdrop to a French mirror from the 1920s; a black leather chair by Fritz Heningson; a contemporary lamp with a walnut veneer shade by Leif Recke; a low chair that was custom made in 1950 by Vladamir Kagan; a Japanese root sculpture; and inside the arch, a copper seed pod sculpture by Richard Savage.

ABOVE At the far end below the window, a Reed-designed Corian sink stands on a bespoke oak table that matches the breakfast bar nearby.

OPPOSITE Shielded by a two-thirds height screen, the bedroom zone is flanked by two fireplaces, each with modern brushed-steel fire surrounds. The bedside cabinets are steel utility pieces from the United States, and the plaster relief of a French soldier is mounted on a square painted on the wall.

THOMAS DE CRUZ

THE UNUSUAL SHAPE of the garden, lined by two streets, gave rise to this spectacular extension in Shepherds Bush. Not wanting to compromise either the south elevation of the building, nor the length of the garden to the west, the architects came up with the idea of wrapping the new extension around the existing building in a glazed curve.

The main concept of the scheme was concerned with maximizing natural light, taking advantage of the path of the sun. Unlike many other extensions or conservatories that have a roof falling toward the perimeter, the idea here was to go skyward. With the roof sloping up and outward, the feeling of space was dramatically enhanced as the new transparent doors ceased to represent the termination point of one's view. Through expansive views of sky and treetops, the meaning of extending the house into the garden is much more fully explored.

The rear walls of the old building were demolished, with a steel frame on two pad foundations now supporting the first-floor level. To gain height and enable a lofty, sloping ceiling, the floor of the above bathroom was raised, and the exterior was clad in copper to match the wooden floors inside.

OPPOSITE AND BELOW Two oversized and tapered columns and blond woodwork give the space a nautical feel, and the cooking and preparation area of the kitchen, fitted around one of the columns, is lit from the north-facing overhead windows. Through sliding glass doors, the extension opens up almost entirely from south to west, adding an uncluttered lightness to the internal space and integrating the garden into the living room. The hardwood deck outside increases the space both visually and practically and gives it a sympathetic base upon which to stand.

RIGHT In the enormous new expansion, the family can relax, sit, play, or eat at the big table, placed right in front of the main doors. From the entrance, the direction of the pale floorboards leads the eye straight out to the garden.

DEREK WYLIE
ARCHITECTS

THIS HOUSE in Clerkenwell, originally a nineteenth-century silversmith's workshop, is on the western fringe of the Financial City and close to Smithfield Market and the Barbican Centre. Clerkenwell was a thriving artisan quarter for over a hundred years that rapidly declined in the 1950s, but has since attracted new urban development and a young, fashionable population.

The building had undergone numerous transformations and had become a rundown venue for impromptu raves when the owner bought the 4,844-square-foot (450 m²) property and commissioned Derek Wylie Architects to devise a scheme.

The clients wanted a modern solution that would also embrace the rough-and-tumble aspects of family life with two young boys. The resulting interiors allow the free flow of movement and light between living spaces and a new courtyard, which forms the focus of the L-shaped design. At the same time, to contribute to development costs, the owners wanted to split the site into two units (one of which could be sold) and to allow space for an office that would be separate from the home, yet visually connected to it. A complex program, but one that was totally satisfied by this solution—a family home that occupies the entire ground footprint of the site plus the rear first-floor workshop area and basement—a total of 2,691 square feet (250 m²) of floor space.

The new construction is deliberately durable to withstand the wear and tear of family life, with precise detailing to contrast with the roughness of the existing shell. A new boarded oak floor has been laid throughout the ground level, including the stepped entrance ramp, to emphasize the continuous spatial flow from the front entrance to the rear courtyard. Similarly, limestone spreads from the courtyard into the kitchen and dining areas. Radiant heat has been installed in the stone floor for comfort.

LEFT Despite the modern design, the feeling of the original building seems to remain through the use of natural materials, the original brickwork, and the glimpses through windows and rooflights of the surrounding neighborhood.

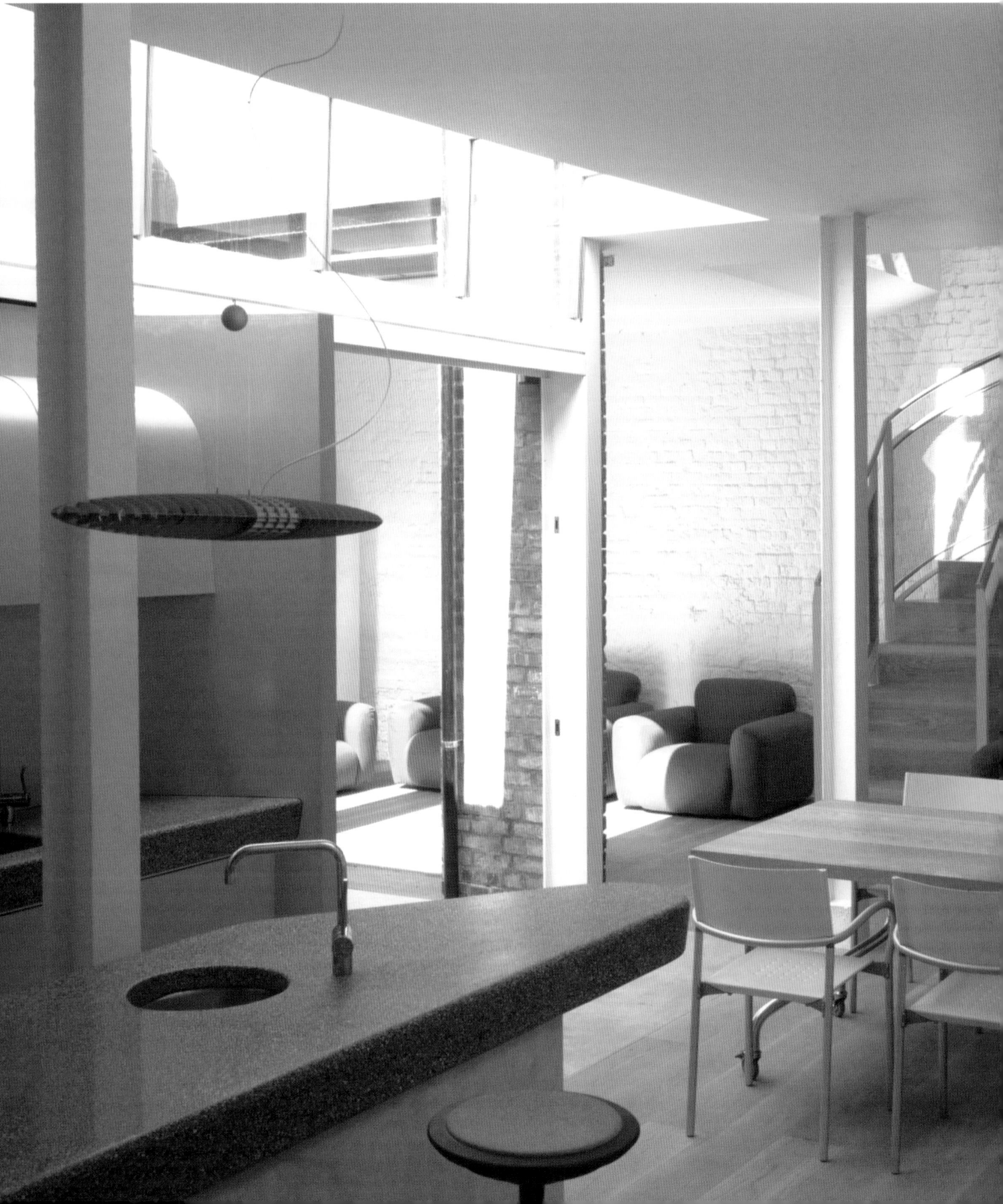

LEFT The kitchen structure is a continuous, free-standing wall that wraps to enclose units, countertops, and equipment, but also provides a concealed slot for the 8-foot (2.4-meter) square sliding door. The wall is constructed using .25-inch (6-mm) plywood formed on metal studs and clad in aluminum. Gull-wing doors on the upper-level cabinets maximize daylight from the rooflight above to the counter tops below. The counters are specially formed from terrazzo with shaped ends to aid movement. Natural glass-reinforced cement, which is particularly resistant to impact, was used for the island unit.

ABOVE Each of the new staircases has been placed to suggest physical separation between different living areas without corrupting the continuity of the space. Each has 50mm thick oak steps, and the rear staircase uses a cantilevered, stepped edge plate, supported by a full-height mast which tapers towards its fixing positions at ground and roof truss level. Guarding is provided by steel weave mesh normally used for sieving and grading stones, but which has the quality of adjusting its grid to the angle and curve of the stair.

ABOVE AND RIGHT The basement bathroom was conceived as an area in which to linger, hence a control link to the media den at the ground floor level. The vanity top is also fabricated from limestone with an integral trough at one end, supported by a cantilevered mild steel frame concealed beneath.

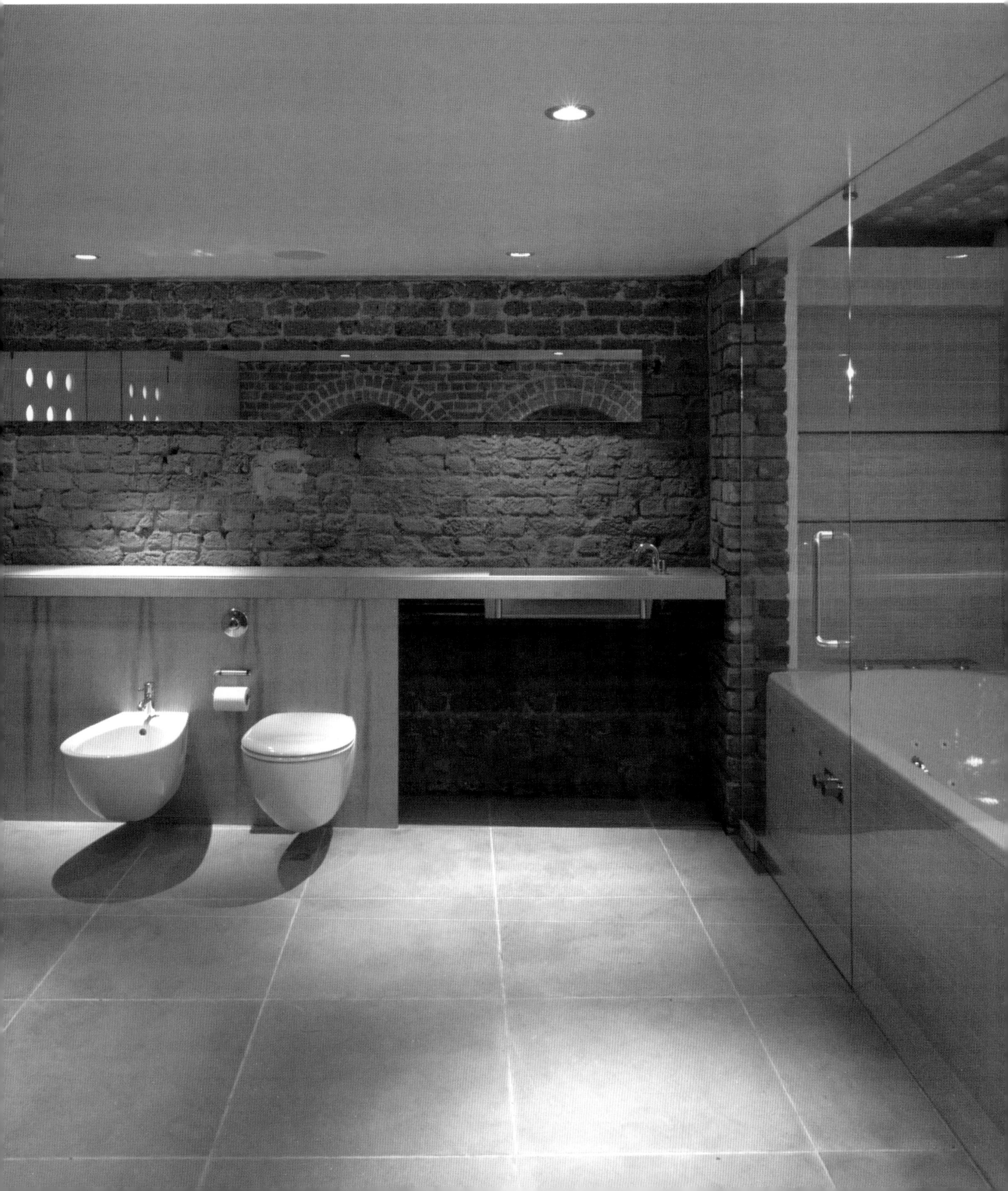

ROLAND
COWAN

THOUGH THE PREDOMINANT feel in this house is modern, uncluttered, and pared down, the architects at Roland Cowan admit that their inspiration for some of the colors and finishes came from the church across the road. The view of its rubble-stone walls dominated the front of the first-floor reception room, and sunlight reflected off the stained glass window, so Roland Cowan and their team used the stone tones in the finish of the architectural insertions, such as the polished plaster fireplace. The walls were painted in a totally matte, hand-mixed distemper that allowed other objects to stand out.

The original first floor was subdivided into four rooms including a kitchen and bathroom, so all these partitions were removed, and a new scheme was generated around an L-shaped reception room—with elements such as television, stereo, toy cupboard and stairs, all hidden behind 11-foot- (3.4 m) high swivel doors.

Utilizing a long, narrow space, the kitchen also has hidden secrets—such as a frameless door from the dining room that, when closed, abuts a plate of glass beside the wall of windows, and creates a physical separation between the two rooms, without losing the advantage of the elegant Victorian-style glazing.

RIGHT AND FOLLOWING PAGES Though most of the original features—plaster moldings and shutter-boxed sash windows—were retained as a record of the property's age, the element that dominates the first-floor room is the newly formed storage wall with its floor-to-ceiling coromandel veneered doors.

OPPOSITE AND ABOVE Making maximum use of the view, a wall of units against the window includes a sink and tub. All the units in the kitchen were designed by Roland Cowan and the steel framing and continuous steel countertop, which wraps down on the dining room junction to frame a side-access cutlery drawer unit that projects through the junction plane, was made by Gec Anderson.

AUKETT
TYTHERLEIGH

THOUGH THE VIEW from this high-level duplex apartment in Central London is spectacular, the space was incredibly difficult to work with. Graham Tytherleigh, who was responsible for the interior, explains that the building was designed on the golden section, like a spiral, so that although all the windows have a graceful curve, every space was an awkward triangular segment. In fact, to achieve this space, the owner, a senior city director relocating from California, bought two units, one above the other, so the architects were able to cut away the floor and expand vertically. Even so, they had to create the illusion that the apartment was larger than it was by concealing all the storage, avoiding any formal cupboards with handles, and not putting any artworks on the walls. The only exception is the series of six niches to hold the owner's miniature chair collection. Fortunately, she had discarded all previous possessions. So Aukett Tytherleigh were free to choose timeless classic furniture with simple, unfussy shapes, and supplement them with pieces of their own design—such as the bed, bedroom storage, and dining table.

LEFT In the difficult curved space, the architects tried to keep all the elements as calm as possible, combining pale colors and natural materials such as limestone, oak, and glass in the helical stair that links the two levels.

TOP Upstairs, the sleeping area has a low screen and a lowered ceiling. An architect-designed headboard and bedside tables follow the curvilinear theme. The curtains, a double layer of sheer fabric, close at the push of a button to encircle the bed.

BOTTOM Along one wall of the downstairs space, the kitchen combines a simple stainless steel freestanding island unit with a raised limestone screen. Behind it, utensils are hidden within a false partition, fronted by dark-blue lacquered panels whose simple rectangular pattern were meant to suggest a modern abstract painting.

OPPOSITE Like many compositions of circles and curving spirals, the elements inside the space echo the nautilus shape of the building and even the elegant dome of nearby St. Paul's Cathedral.

SIMON CONDER

THE ARCHITECTURAL SOLUTION for the transformation of
this building was developed not on the drawing board or
the computer, but from an early discussion between Simon
Conder and his clients that took place while they were
sitting on top of the roof. Conder's clients, a musician and
a cook, had bought the top two floors of the Holland Park
fire station and found themselves with a number of small,
badly lit rooms with small windows. So they wanted an
imaginative way of transforming the rather depressing
environment into a light and exciting new home that would
have a generosity of scale and spirit. More specifically,
they wanted an open-floor-plan living area centered around
the kitchen; three bedrooms, one with en-suite bathroom
and one that doubled as a study; an additional bathroom;
and most importantly, plenty of built-in storage for their
large music collection. The dramatic views out over West
London made it clear that the nineteenth-century building
could be transformed if its rooftop potential could be
exploited to create an additional living space that also let
light down into the center of the deep, dark structure.

OPPOSITE A view of the stairs that was one of the keys to the architects'
solution. From the newly formed roof, light pours down the pale channel, a
combination of unpainted hard plaster and Portland stone. On the right, the
curved wall pinches space out of the void and allocates it to double-height
storage on the other side.

ABOVE From the top floor, a second stair (this one in sandblasted glass with a galvanized steel frame) leads up to the rooftop conservatory. A floor of American white oak links the kitchen and living room, where light seems to be creeping in from every direction.

OPPOSITE In the top-floor living room, a wall of storage in birch plywood provides plenty of space for the owners records and CDs, and a glazed panel in the floor lets the daylight that filters in from the slated roof above continue its way to the hallway below. As a final touch, an enormous mirror on the end wall heightens the perception of space still further.

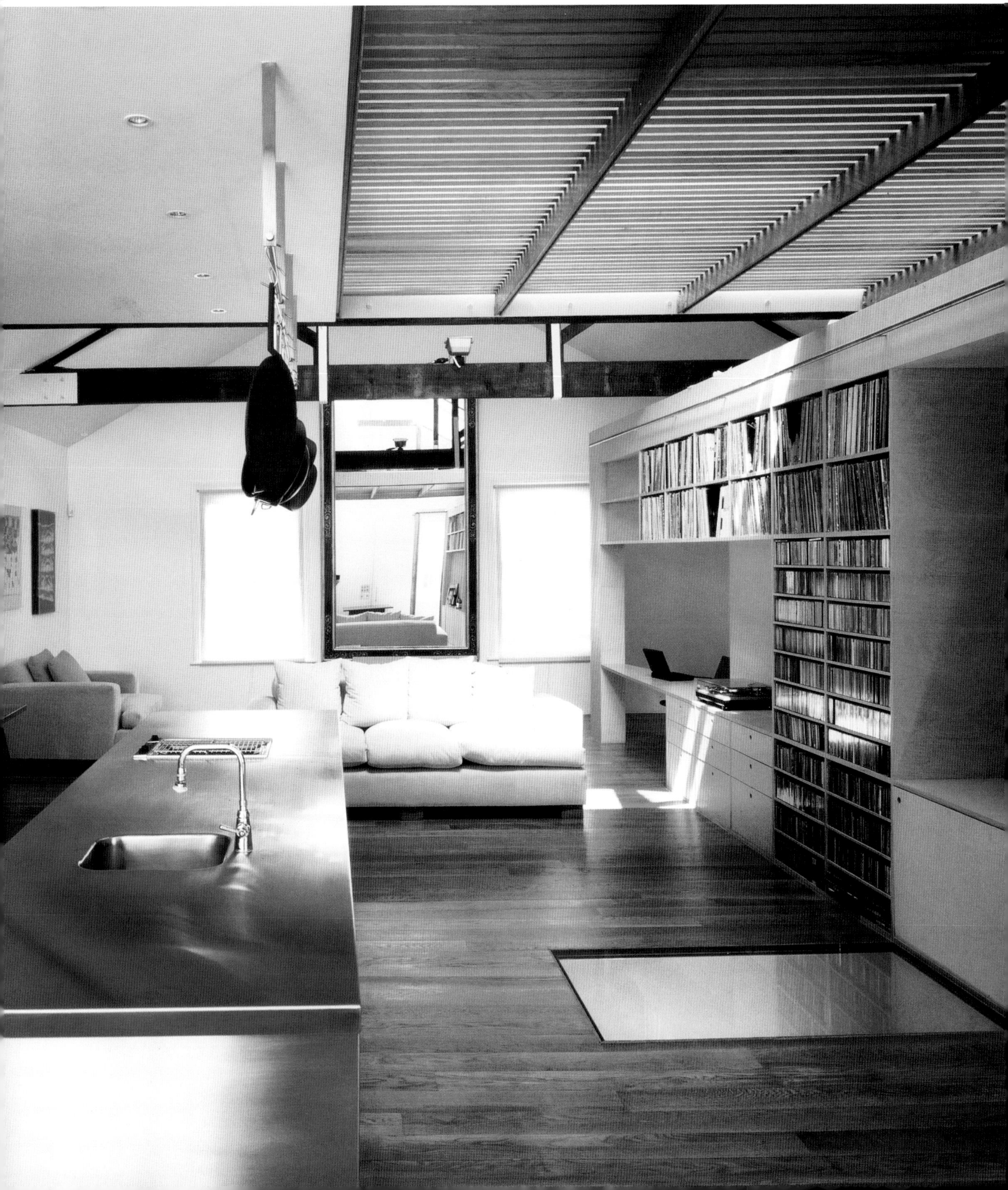

ABOVE Within the roof space, the newly created conservatory has a double glazed roof that can retract in good weather to become an open terrace.

OPPOSITE The master bathroom walls are all laminated and tempered glass, and the tub was purposely designed and constructed in cedar.

POWELL-TUCK
ASSOCIATES

IN THE PAST, London has been accused of turning its back on the Thames. But with the conversion of many of the old warehouses, and the creation of interesting new buildings, apartments with a view of London's famous river are now as sought after as such rooms are in Paris.

The owners of this space sold their 10,000-square-foot (930 m²) country house on Kingston Hill, to move to one of the upper floors of Sir Norman Foster's Riverside One Building. They asked architects Powell-Tuck Associates, who had worked on their other house, to convert what was once two adjoining apartments into one home where they could have the entire family stay. The owners measured all the parts of the country house they actually used, to make sure they would have exactly the same amount of space when they moved.

The space was designed to be elegantly contemporary for clients who did not want their interior to dominate their lives or compromise their traditional notion of comfort. It was further configured to provide a large amount of storage, a major concern when moving from a larger house to a smaller one.

One space flows into another but can be closed down by concealed wall panels to allow varying levels of privacy. The master bedroom is positioned to face the sunrise over Albert Bridge. Materials were carefully selected to convey calm—stone, timber, and glass dominate, but were softened by soft textures and a huge carpet, which was made in Hong Kong and delivered in one piece by river crane, another advantage of living beside the Thames.

RIGHT Custom-designed lights provide discreet, low-level illumination, especially when the lights are dimmed and the apartment soaks in the magical view of the river and the bridge at Battersea.

ABOVE AND RIGHT The kitchen was supplied by Bulthaup, but was integrated
into architectural composition using specially designed cupboards.

OPPOSITE AND TOP LEFT The stone in the master bedroom and bathroom was prepared to the architect's specification.

TOP RIGHT AND BOTTOM Powell-Tuck Associates designed all the lighting and key architectural pieces of furniture. The soft furniture came mainly from Bruno Triplet and Christian Liaigre.

MICHAEL
REEVES

FROM AN UNPROMISING, rather vertical London house with a dismal underground complex of rooms and dozens of doors, Michael Reeves and his team have created something that looks neither English nor Mediterranean, but that has its roots in both cultures. The spectacular centerpiece has become the skylit atrium dining room, with its electronically operated glass roof, gently turning staircase, and oversized oxidized-aluminum planters, each one containing a live olive tree. The undeniably tailored look of the whole house is a clever and deceivingly simple mix of expensive antiques and pieces from Habitat and Ikea, and the at-first-sight monochromatic palette is, in fact, a combination of many colors, from white to cream, warm taupe to honey. Reeves believes that a neutral scheme provides an ideal base to which inhabitants may add additional colors.

LEFT AND OPPOSITE Reeves took out all the interconnecting doors and internal windows and replaced the dog-leg stair with an elegant tour de force in limestone and painted plaster. The floor, also in pale limestone, extends up the walls and wraps around the columns to become a skirting.

ABOVE In place of a traditional banister, the designers have filled in the newly formed arches with simple glass panels. The carpet that extends throughout the house is one of the designer's own designs that was made in Spain, and, together with many of the other pieces, is available commercially.

OPPOSITE TOP AND BOTTOM In the more formal first-floor drawing room, the curtains can be closed to extend along one entire wall, and the furnishings— many available from Reeves' own London store—are a combination of traditional and contemporary. The Christian Liagre sofa is framed by oversized table lamps with wenge stained ash bases, and the cartwheel, one of a pair beside the fireplace, is from China. At the opposite end **(BOTTOM)** the custom-made daybed is by Hitch Mylius and the framed metallic panels, along with the 1950s vases, are from New York.

RIGHT TOP AND BOTTOM The birchwood paneling that totally encloses the bedroom also conceals the wardrobes. The two bedside trunks and console table were designed by Reeves. The two suede stools at the end of the bed are from Habitat.

OPPOSITE Though the state-of-the-art bathtub and sink were bought from a London supplier with their matching tall cabinet, they seem tailor made for the house, and have been grounded by the ceramic wall tiles and laminated split bamboo flooring. Plumbing is hidden in the custom-designed console that includes a glass shelf. Through the frosted glass wall, two doors lead to a bathroom, with a bidet, sink, large shower, and steam room.

TIMNEY
FOWLER

HAVING MADE A NAME producing fabrics and wallpapers with enlarged eighteenth-century, black-and-white engravings, this husband-and-wife team have recently redesigned their home—a late nineteenth-century double-fronted villa in West London—using a rich and exotic palette. But black, their signature hue, still seems to underpin every room, sometimes outlining the architecture, sometimes brought out in a fireplace, a sofa, or a giant sideboard. Rather than English and Continental, their influences extend to Africa, North America, and the Vienna Secession. The living room colors were inspired by the couple's collection of mid-nineteenth-century ceramics and pottery, showcased on an aesthetic-movement ebonized oak sideboard, and then mixed on site.

Set on creating a contemporary environment with updated period references, Sue Timney completely restored and redecor-ated the house, tearing out one of the rear sash windows and extending the living room into a custom-built conservatory/kitchen, where dark green is used to outline the wooden roof frame. The walls were covered in reclaimed late-nineteenth-century pine to make it feel like a modern lodge.

BELOW AND OPPOSITE All set on an undertreated floor of African slate, the furniture in the conservatory/kitchen includes a 1930s leather sofa with seat cushions newly covered in Harris tweed, a set of original chairs by Heals & Sons circa 1930, and a Gothic-style central console. On the walls, the plates are a mixture of Fornasetti and Timney Fowler, and the large painting is mid-twentieth-century English silk screen.

OPPOSITE AND ABOVE Though seemingly a riot of periods, shapes, and colors, the living room ingredients have been carefully composed and held together by the couple's use of black. At the epicenter is the inspirational pottery and ceramics collection, balanced by the restored fireplace, one of the house's original features. All the cushions and fabrics are by Timney Fowler.

OPPOSITE Grids, checks, and frames were the inspiration for the master bed-room, where a gallery of family photographs forms a backdrop to the black lacquer bed. Timney Fowler's fabric is used on the bed and at the window.

ABOVE The horizontal-stripe, light gray wallpaper, specially designed for the house, is used in the front hall and extends up the staircase to the first floor, combined with a vertical black and gray companion, from a London paint and wallpaper specialist.

MATTHEW PRIESTMAN

RETHINKING THE FUNCTION and the layout of rooms in a house is something that most people don't have to deal with when they move to a new property. Usually, they base their ideas on what they see and, in fact, choose a home on that basis. For the owner of this house, it was the area and the quiet aspect, plus the building's potential, which attracted him. Despite the fact that it was in a conservation area, he was still free to make certain structural changes inside—so long as he kept the garage intact.

From a lineup of several top architectural companies, the owner chose Matthew Priestman for the job, and together they set about a radical rethink of the double-fronted mews house. The traditional plan, with the living area on the ground floor and bedrooms upstairs, was reversed with guest/children's bedrooms on the street level, living/dining area and kitchen on the first floor, and private quarters—a study, master bedroom and bathroom—on the second floor. Finally, the three levels were tied together by an open stair that exposed the whole height of the building and greatly increased the flow of space and daylight.

PREVIOUS SPREAD LEFT Hugging the wall, the new stair, with its oak treads, slices right up to the top floor in one sweep, concealing, on the ground floor, storage and a small bathroom, and allowing daylight to penetrate deep into the building. The first-floor landing has a glass bridge and a glass wall to increase opacity.

PREVIOUS SPREAD RIGHT All the furniture in the living space is blocked and rectilinear, and though the colors vary, the scheme holds together. Above the non-functioning fireplace, an integral screen for video projection and steel mesh speakers are concealed behind panels where once the chimney breast would have been.

OPPOSITE The kitchen can be screened off by lowering and closing a slim gray venetian blind, and a pocket door that slides back into the wall when not required. The dining table was designed by Priestman.

ABOVE Light washes across the wall and ceiling planes in the kitchen from a narrow glass panel in the floor above a painting and a flush light box set into the wall beside it.

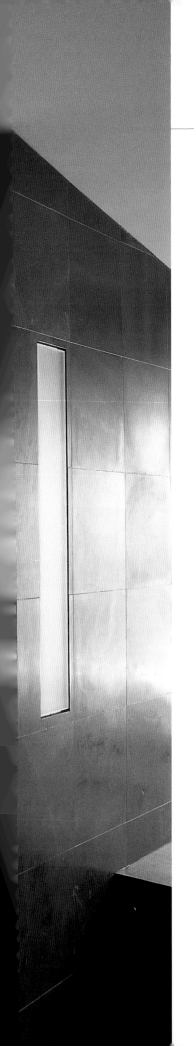

OPPOSITE AND ABOVE In the adjoining master bathroom, all the walls and floor are clad with slate. Smooth 12-inch (300 mm) square tiles contrast with a rough hewn variation that is washed from above by a long, thin skylight created to emphasize the texture. A narrow, red cedar bench links the shower to the bathroom and one entire wall of mirror **(BEHIND THE SINK)**, and greatly compensates for the feeling of claustrophobia that the low, sloping ceiling might have given.

BROOKES STACEY RANDALL

FACED WITH an enormous 3,000-square-foot (279 m²) empty loft, and a client who wants an apartment with a sense of fun and a place that visitors will feel comfortable, Brookes Stacey Randall created this space.

The brief was to provide a master bedroom with en-suite bathroom, a guest bedroom with its own shower room, an office, a laundry area, a kitchen, dining and living areas, and plenty of storage. But instead of placing all these zones together in the center of the space, they decided to put them near the front entrance.

The strategy within this private area was to break down the notion of corridors and rooms with wall surfaces of contrasting color, texture, and opacity, while meeting the fire codes and leaving the maximum open space beyond.

Located below the south-facing, eye-level window, the kitchen was seen as the social hub of the apartment. It is the only fixed insertion into the space. Cooking and preparing drinks become a social activity, with the host never distanced from his guests. Eventually, the client will add a dining table and a pool table, so the architects have created two dropped areas of ceiling to delineate these activities, without any visual disruption or physical obstruction. Space, light, function, and flexibility seem to be the cornerstones to the scheme, to which the architects add tranquillity, leaving the client to provide the fun.

RIGHT AND OPPOSITE The entrance is compressed. It passes from the front door between a gray-green storage wall and the terra-cotta box of the guest shower room. Beyond, the area lightens and widens, and the ceiling steps up. Daylight is diffused through the curved, toughened, etched-glass wall of the main bathroom. Wide double doors provide access to the main space, whose scale is accentuated in contrast to the constricted approach.

ABOVE On the third floor of the former warehouse building, this vast space was kept open, with only the existing columns and beams and two lowered ceiling panels left to define the zones.

OPPOSITE The spacious kitchen area includes three freestanding elements. A sink and dishwasher are concealed below the windows. On the right is a unit with built-in range that has open storage for kitchen equipment below and extra width for serving food, and along the front are the oven and cantilevered table.

OPPOSITE The master bedroom, complete with glass doors to its own bathroom, is located on the east to maximize morning light.

ABOVE The bathroom was conceived as a place of calm—almost a retreat. The shower, in the center of the room, falls to a center drain without a screen or shower curtain. The curved-glass walls allow daylight to penetrate into the space, which is supplemented at night by floor lights.

ARCHITEAM

THERE ARE TWO WAYS to create more space in an interior, according to architectural designer Nico Rensch. One is with the spacial treatment itself—creating new doors, larger windows, using space to its maximum. The other is by tricking the mind—simplifying or taking away unnecessary details and giving the mind less information to digest. This trick of minimalism—what Rensch calls maximalism—is the theme of every Architeam client's brief. But the fewer things you use, the better they must be designed and detailed. This house seems to be the textbook example of Rensch's philosophy, but it wasn't a very inspiring start.

The owners, a journalist and a computer consultant, had bought a very narrow cottage in Wandsworth in South London. (It's what Londoners call a "two-up-two-down" house, two rooms on each floor and a staircase in the middle). They wanted the space to emulate a French Chateau, a challenging feat for such a space. Rensch was able to extract a few key elements such as the flooring and the quality of light, but to start, he had to eliminate as much as possible. All the furniture had to go and the clients' lifestyle had to be totally changed. At the same time, Rensch opened up the building—removing walls in the center, so you could "feel" the width of the house as well as see out into the garden. Finally, he treated all the spaces the same, with white walls and dark woodwork.

LEFT Where once were separate little rooms, spaces now flow into each other, and thanks to the new tall windows and doors, the rooms are flooded with light. In the living room, an ogee-profile sandstone surround fireplace was added, and a leCorbusier chair re-covered in brown leather.

OPPOSITE Newly formed French windows now bring the garden into the dining room, where the furniture, as with all the woodwork in the house, was designed and made by Ben Fowler-Contol. The table has a zinc top, and the Dominic chairs are named after Fowler's son.

ABOVE Rensch re-clad the original narrow stair with American walnut– simplifying one side by adding a low wall into which he set low voltage spot lights beside every third tread. On the left, a space that once led to the dining room has now become a closet.

RIGHT Upstairs, a monumental piece of cabinetry by Ben Fowler lines the wall opposite the bed and, as elsewhere, small leather tabs replace normal door and drawer handles.

OPPOSITE In the kitchen, as in the rest of the house, all the woodwork and cabinetry is in American walnut. But unlike normal practice where veneer is laid vertically in a "bookmark repeat," Rensch used a random, more natural approach and laid the panels horizontally. The door fronts of the island unit are finished in child-friendly blackboard paint.

TOP Wide double doors lead from the living room into the kitchen. Throughout, the floor is of limestone the color of milky coffee and the lighting has been kept almost invisibly discreet.

BOTTOM Generous window seats along the wall in both the living room and the kitchen contain storage drawers for toys.

PETER WADLEY

WITHIN THE EXISTING columns and steel beams of this robust former factory building at Chiswick Green in West London, brilliant colors and natural materials make subtle nautical references. Wadley begins each project with a basic rationale that, no matter how obscure, connects to the building and gives meaning to each architectural decision. Following a criteria checklist, his planning process considers all the constraints and the client's wishes, and, by combining design ideas that are related to a storyline—in this case sail-making, wooden floors, boats, and navigation—allows the interior architecture to interlock and be read as a cohesive whole. The basic nautical justification came from the architect's memories of a sail-makers' loft in Cowes on the Isle of Wight. Wadley made a definite decision to paint all the new walls in the entrance hall dark gray so that the space contrasted with the lighter living areas beyond and set off the colors of the other design elements—a curved "lighthouse" with a porthole, powder-blue curved panels like the starboard side of a yacht, and the rudder-shaped pivot-door that leads into the bedroom.

RIGHT Taking maximum advantage of the sunlight that floods in from the large corner windows, the small study and the living room retain most of the original factory-size features. When the large foldaway doors are left open, the living room can become an extension to the bedroom.

ABOVE LEFT In the dining area the large six-seat table has a scrubbed wooden top that echoes the maple wood floor—a new addition that extends throughout the space.

ABOVE RIGHT Vibrant colors inspired by navigational buoys that lead ships into harbor emphasize the newly created walls and the curved lighthouse-inspired enclosure conceals a third bedroom.

OPPOSITE The small galley kitchen also reflects boating proportions. The slightly curving door with its spinnaker-shaped handle, is made in cherry wood.

RIGHT The master bedroom—seen from the living room—was positioned in the eastern end of the building, where it gets the morning light. The headboard and night tables were made from cherry wood and match the cabinetry in the kitchen.

DOUGLAS STEPHEN
PARTNERSHIP

OVER THE PAST 10 YEARS, the single most radical development in the housing industry has been the loft conversion. Property developers have been aggressively buying up empty or derelict commercial spaces all over London and converting them into "shell" units—that is to say, with plug-in points for services, but no partitions or finishes, leaving the purchasers and their architect free to tailor-make individual apartments.

This space, with 600 square feet (56 m²) on the entry level and 450 square feet (42 m²) on the mezzanine, is part of the last stage of an enormous Thameside development called Bankside Lofts, and is the latest of over twenty loft fit-outs that the Douglas Stephen Partnership has done for various clients. On this occasion, the owner was a young investment banker fed up with commuting to and from his office in the business district around St. Paul's Cathedral, and who can now walk to work. His brief for this rather unusually shaped unit with windows on three sides was to maximize the space and the views, while providing a two-bedroom apartment. Simon Colebrook, assisted by Adrian Ball, investigated many different layouts before deciding on this solution in which all the elements are turned toward the spectacular view of St. Paul's. Downstairs, the stainless steel bar, cooking and eating areas; and upstairs, an extra seating area, bedroom corridor, and even the bathtub, share this perfect vista.

RIGHT The predominantly white color scheme was chosen to enhance the natural colors of the high-quality materials—maple flooring and benches, limestone floor tiles, stainless steel worktops, and sandblasted glass doors and screens.

OPPOSITE The kitchen and breakfast bar were placed on a raised platform of limestone tiles that incorporates all the services. The Tryptich painting was specially commissioned from Amanda Marshall.

ABOVE On the upper level, a second sitting area is reached by a steel and glass staircase with maple treads. A glass balustrade continues up and along the edge of the curved mezzanine and makes maximum use of the light.

OPPOSITE Downstairs, sliding panels can be closed to create a private study and second bedroom, while upstairs, the window into the bathroom can also be closed by a sliding glass panel.

OPPOSITE One of the strongest uses of color is introduced on the mosaic-tiled shower cylinder adjacent to the master bedroom.

ABOVE The window into the bathroom gives a tubside view of the panorama.

ARTHUR
COLLIN

ALL-WHITE INTERIORS are a contemporary cliché. In practice, there is no such thing as a standard white. Any particular white is not necessarily the same as any other white. This project embraces the subtle differences that plague color matching by adopting a color scheme that uses three very subtly different whites.

Most unusually, the inspiration came not from the drawing board but from the bathroom, where the exact whites used were determined by the selection of wall tiling, which is a handmade mosaic using three types of standard, inexpensive white tiles from D.I.Y. stores—Homebase white, B&Q white, and Texas white. The differences between these whites achieve a subtle decorative effect that results in a warmth impossible with white minimalism.

This project comprised the complete refurbishment of the top half of a Georgian terrace house into a two-bedroom apartment. The house had been completely gutted and rebuilt in the 1970s and so it was possible to insert a completely contemporary interior without being encumbered with original features of historic value. The interior was opened up to create a living space with a sense of openness and lightness, and continuity from one side to another.

The theme of different whites is carried through the apartment on cabinetry colored in the three shades of white. The doors, drawer fronts, and shutters have an irregular layout that ignores the arrangement of the cabinets behind. They use a series of slots in place of handles to provide access and the resultant surface, while smooth and monolithic, has an unusual texture and geometry that even extends to the window shutters. In contrast, one wall of the living room has an open walnut shelf with a paintinglike arrangement of books that forms a patchwork of colors and textures.

RIGHT TOP In the kitchen, one countertop is formed from a single L-shaped piece of stainless steel measuring 8 feet by 8 feet (2.4 x 2.4m) with integral sinks. Extending into the living area, the other units are topped by a piece of fine rubbed-back Welsh slate. The removable circular breakfast table has a top formed from recycled-plastic detergent bottles—pieces of red, yellow, blue, green, and white bottles can be seen within the surfaces, along with the odd fragment of barcode and label.

RIGHT BOTTOM Looking toward the kitchen, the dining table is surrounded by contemporary chairs by Marc Newson for Morosco. The staircase bookcase is a stack of thirteen odd-sized boxes in three shades of white that rises two stories in place of the stair balustrade and handrails.

FOLLOWING PAGES In the living room, the furniture is an eclectic mixture of contemporary pieces, twentieth-century classics, and antiques. On the floor, a Normandy cow hide rug covers part of the oiled solid American walnut floor. The paneled window shutters allow various grades of privacy and natural lighting using different open/closed combinations. In their open position against the wall, small integral panels fold down to form display shelves.

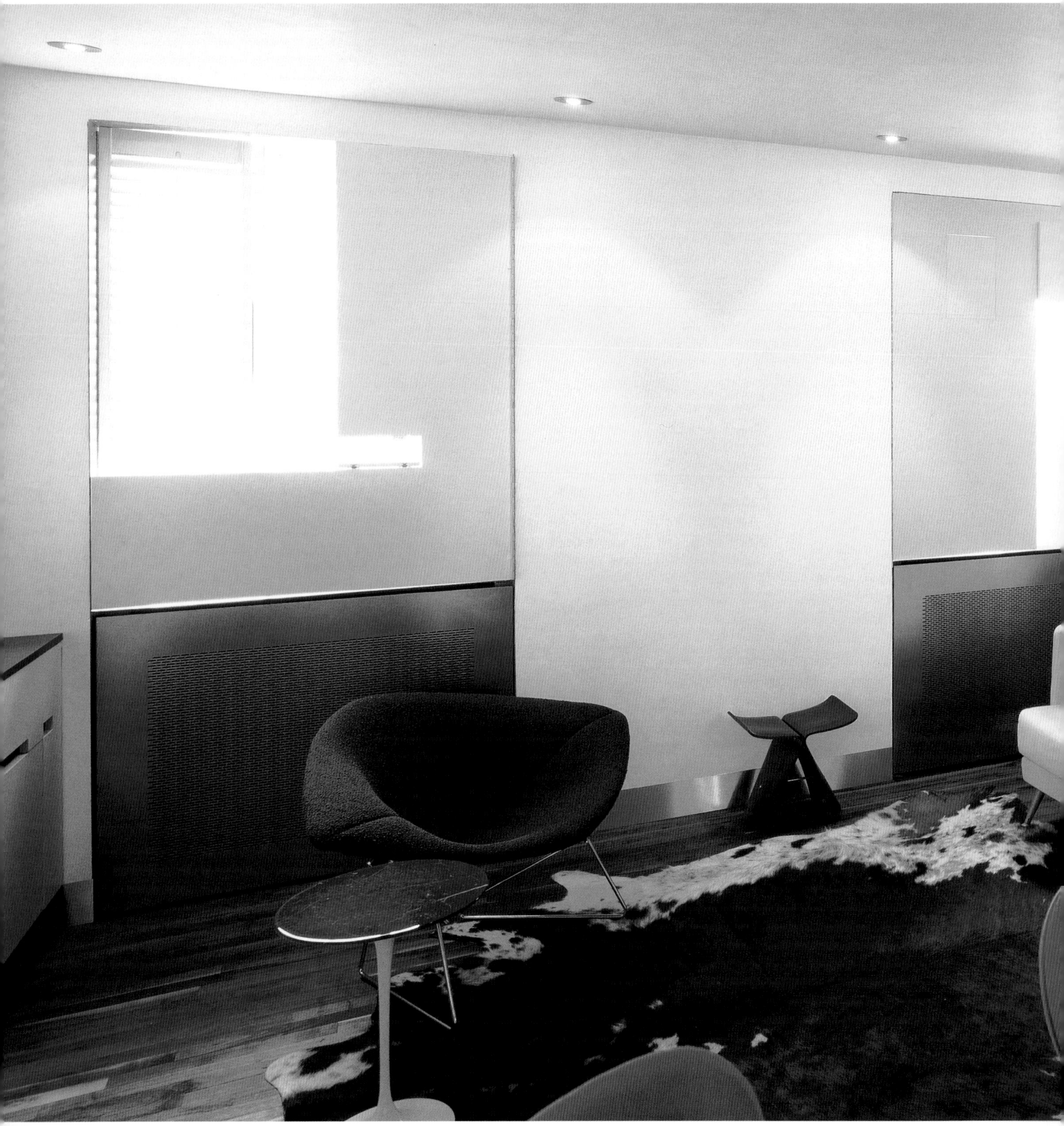

AZMAN
OWENS

THIS LATE GEORGIAN terrace house is located in a historically significant neighborhood near Waterloo and the South Bank. These Grade II listed, cottage-like terraces characteristically have small, dark rooms with little in the way of adequate kitchen or bathroom facilities.

The clients both lead high-profile lifestyles in fashion and the arts so the architects, Ferhan Azman and Joyce Owens, responded to their requirements by creating a simple, engaging living environment as an antidote to an often hectic lifestyle.

The decision was made to replace the ramshackle lean-to at the rear with a light and pristine structure, which is clearly distinct from the existing cottage. This glass and steel extension houses the kitchen on the ground floor and bathroom on the first floor. To the existing building, narrow slots have been cut in the ground floor to allow daylight into the basement and similar narrow windows succeed in opening out the whole house.

OPPOSITE Adjoining the kitchen, the small Georgian dining room has been brought into the 20th century by painting out all the architectural features and the addition of contemporary art works around the foil-topped table. The cardboard dining chairs were designed by David Bartlett.

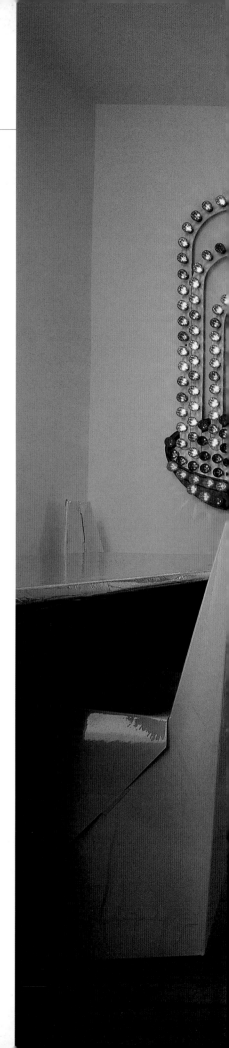

OPPOSITE From the rear of the house, the newly inserted glass and steel box does not attempt to match the rest of the building, though on closer examination, windows line up and doors old and new match in size and proportion.

ABOVE Brought from the client's family home in Gloucestershire, the cobbles used in the garden have been continued into the kitchen, where the stainless steel unit—placed against the glass—has been kept open to match the feeling of spatial continuity.

RIGHT TOP AND BOTTOM The top floor of the new addition to the house, contains a glass and mirror bathroom. Mirrors behind the basin reflect the steel mesh wall—a contemporary reference to Turkish shutters—that open from the bottom and, like their wooden counterparts, are used to provide an element of privacy. The translucent glass benchtop allows the client to display her cosmetics underneath.

RIGHT BOTTOM The bathtub—designed by Azman Owens—is also in glass, with only the two ends in teak. White rollerblinds can be drawn for additional privacy.

MALIN
IOVINO

SOME PEOPLE'S IDEA of a dream kitchen is dark wood paneling, an aga cooker, a big pine table, and roses around the door. But since the 1980s, the kitchen is no longer considered as a separate room, away from the rest of the house, but has become the focus of family life, whose dinner guests can be a part of the cooking process, happy to join in, or stay on after meals relaxing and chatting around the table. Even professional chefs have joined the trend, removing a wall of their kitchen and opening their restaurants up for the entertainment and inspiration of diners.

When Swedish interior designer Malin Iovino and her husband had the opportunity to expand the top floor of their London warehouse apartment to incorporate a vacant apartment next door, her first thought was to have an enormous kitchen/eating/living area that took up the whole floor. To achieve her dream, she first had to gut the existing space-removing a living room, a guest bedroom, a cloakroom, and a kitchen, and the walls of the adjoining purchase.

In this bare seventh floor shell, Iovino accentuated the room's sheer proportions by using bleached colors, pale wood, clean lines, and classically simple, uncluttered details. Along one wall, the designer boxed in the windows and constructed floor-to-ceiling cupboards to hide the uneven alcoves, and match the seamless units opposite. The floor is a combination of twelve-foot lengths of pale maple and cream colored limestone, and the only bold color comes from the two unmatched sofas, and a geometric rug at the far end.

RIGHT A new stair, which Iovino created by adapting an off-the-peg model with new thick Maplewood treads and powder-coated silver metal work, leads down to the guest wing.

OPPOSITE At the far end of the living space, the designer placed sofas on a geometric rug that combines both their colors. Outside the floor-to-ceiling glass doors, a narrow terrace runs the full width of the rec room.

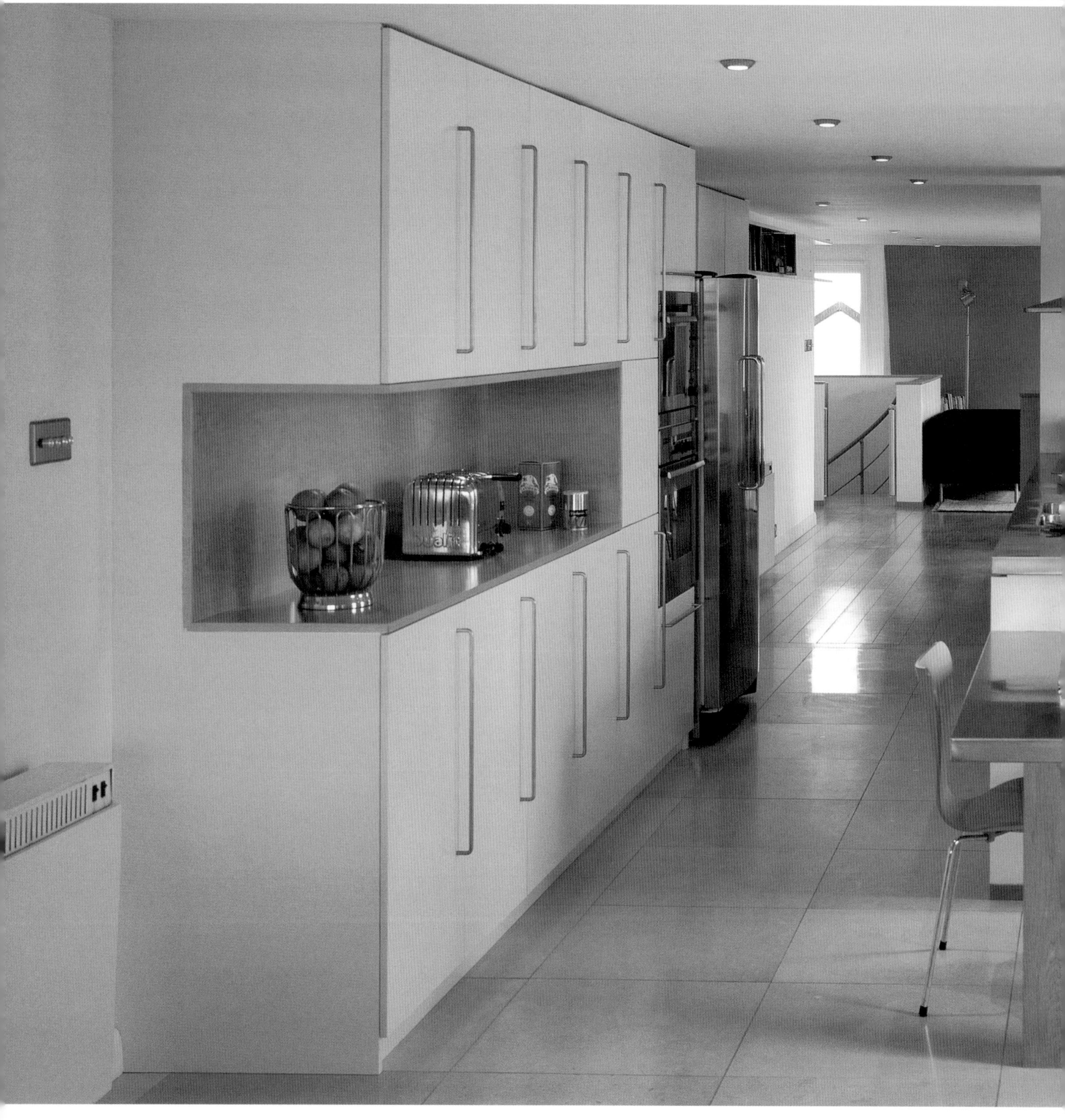

ABOVE Because of the uneven ceiling, the designer left a shadow gap above the wall cupboards and kept all the colors pale to make the height seem greater. At the front end, a seating area for watching TV is placed beside the stairs.

ABOVE In the guest bathroom, the shower alcove is defined by blue mosaic tiles from Domus tile, and separated only by a simple glass wall and a small step. The cupboard was made to Iovino's specification, in maple.

OPPOSITE In the master bedroom, the bed (by Palluccao Italia) was placed not against the wall, but a newly created unit that conceals storage for clothes. Most of the furniture was from Viadict, a London supplier of contemporary designs.

24/Seven Architecture + Design

83A Geffrye Street
London E2 8HX
Tel: 0171 729 9194
Fax: 0171 729 9193
Mob: 0956 653 161/160
E-mail: twentyfour.seven@virgin.net

Graeme Williamson and Zoe Smith at 24/Seven are primarily interested in the reediting of experience, space, materials and their context in a cut-and-paste culture that is in continual reconfiguration. Throughout their work they have used the city as a reference to develop a language that engages with diversity, provoking a review of the cultural coding inherent in social relationships. Generating environments conducive to being creative, productive, and social has been a core motivation. During this time, the partners have worked on retail, office, exhibition, residential, and public spaces as well as a broad range of furniture commissions.

Adjaye and Russell Architecture & Design

24 Sunbury Workshops
Swanfield Street
London E2 7LF
Tel: 0171 739 4969
Fax: 0171 739 3484
E-mail: dadjaye@compuserve.com

David Adjaye and William Russell formed Adjaye and Russell Architecture and Design in 1994 when the two former RCA classmates collaborated on a series of sets for the televised concert "Live at the Lighthouse," commissioned by the AIDS charity London Lighthouse. Their growing list of London/U.K. sites includes commercial and private spaces, and the building of several new contemporary houses. Additionally, they are working on several projects in Europe, Ghana, and the U.S.

Alan Power Architects Ltd.

5 Haydens Place
London W11 1LY
Tel: 0171 229 9375
Fax: 0171 221 4172
E-mail: apa@dircon.co.uk

Alan Power is a design-led practice whose work has ranged from new houses, office interiors, exhibition design, alterations to listed buildings, shop interiors, and new-build offices to the design of light fittings and furniture. They believe in the importance and value of design for their clients and in the importance of pursuing the full detail of projects through to completion.

Architeam

Campfield House
Powder Mill Lane
Battle, East Sussex TN33 054
Tel:/Fax: 01424 777 181

Formed by architectural designer, Nico Rensch, in 1994, Architeam provides international clients with architectural, furniture, product, graphic, and corporate-identity design, with the philosophy of creating the maximum from the minimum through the expression of materials. Architeam forms a team of architects, designers, and project managers who work as necessary with specialist consultants, contractors, and suppliers from conception to completion with close control of schedules and budgets.

The Architects Practice

23 Beacon Hill
London N7 9LY
Tel: 0207 607 3333
Fax: 0207 700 7066
Mob: 0860 463213
E-mail: ArchPractice@Compuserve.com
Web site: www.Architects-Practice.com

The Architects Practice is a small award-winning firm that specializes in designing high-quality, modern insertions in existing and sometimes historic settings. These include both the refurbishment of old properties and the design of new. Set up in 1986 by Simon Foxell, the Practice currently covers residential, commercial, retail, and exhibition design. The Practice maintains a commitment to the principles of modern design, particularly a strong belief in the creative and, if possible, poetic use of materials.

Arthur Collin Architect

1a Berry Place
London EC1V 0JD
Tel: 0171 490 3520
Fax: 0171 490 3521
E-mail: mail@acarch.demon.co.uk
Web site: www.slumberinggiant.co.uk/ac.html

Arthur Collin specializes in residential, retail, leisure, office, and design. They have designed many houses, house extensions, and apartment interiors around London, including a number of loft-style developments. Recently the office won the BDA Innovative Housing Competition. The practice prides itself on being design-led and is characterized by a spirit of consultation and multidisciplinary collaboration. Great care is taken assembling teams appropriate to each project, combining creative, technical, and managerial skills. The key to their success is effective communication with clients and contractors.

Ash Sakula Architects

38 Mount Pleasant
London WC1X 0AN
Tel: 0171 837 9735
Fax: 0171 837 9708
E-mail: info@ashsak.demon.co.uk
Web site: www.ashsak.demon.co.uk

An award-winning architectural practice founded in 1991, Ash Sakula is well-known for solving unusual problems by careful analysis and insightful design and combining cutting-edge innovation with established craft, among other features. They like to work with clients whose ambitions for their projects are high. The work is essentially a fusion of their vision, their clients' vision, and all the energy and confusion of a typical messy London street.

Aukett Tytherleigh Limited

Atlantic Court
77 King's Road
London SW3 4NX
Contact: Graham Tytherleigh
Tel: 0171 352 3622
Fax: 0171 352 7622
E-mail: g.tytherleigh@aukett-consultancy.com

Aukett Tytherleigh Interior Architects design in the private residential, retail, commercial, office, transport, leisure, and pharmaceutical sectors. The company concentrates on understanding client needs and exceeding their expectations, in terms of product service and management.

Azman Owens Architects
8 St. Albans Place
London N1 0NX
Tel: 0171 354 2955
Fax: 0171 354 2966

Established in 1993, Azman Owens practice architecture and interior design for a range of projects that includes a variety of residential and commercial projects, including Canary Wharf Tower and Scottish Equitable Headquarters. Their approach is to create simple, functional, well-made spaces for new installations and to retain the value and integrity of existing buildings when making them into contemporary spaces.

Brookes Stacey Randall
Architects & Technology Consultants
New Hibernia House Winchester Walk
London SE1 9AG
Tel: 0171 403 0707
Fax: 0171 403 0880

Brookes Stacey Randall has an established track record of successfully responding to clients' needs and providing imaginative and inventive responses to project constraints, as demonstrated on a wide variety of award-winning schemes. A tightly focused group of highly committed architects equipped with the latest in information technology and CAD, the partnership became Design Council Registered in 1991 "by virtue of their consistent high standards of project management and design quality."

Carden Cunietti Limited
83 Westbourne Park Road
London W2 5QH
Tel: 0207 229 8559
Fax: 0207 229 8799
E-mail: E@cc-id.demon.co.uk
Shop Tel: 0207 229 8630

Scottish and Canadian design partners Audrey Carden and Eleanora Cunietti run a design-and-build company that takes on interior projects from the foundation to providing a home with all the luxurious creature comforts. Past and current interior projects include Maida Vale bachelor basements and large family houses in Primrose Hill. In 1996, they opened a small shop that prides itself on stocking a mixture of decorative antiques as well as new products from all over the world. Many of their products are exclusive to the shop, ensuring its cutting-edge originality. The stock is a reflection of the eclecticism evident in their interior design work, which boldly yet harmoniously blends the old with the new.

Derek Wylie Architecture
Bon Marche
444 Brixton Road
London SW9 BEJ
Tel: 0207 274 6373
Fax: 0207 274 1449
E-mail: e.studio@wyliearch.demon.co.uk

Formed in 1984, the practice believes in the development of architectural solutions which explore the articulation and expression of construction detail. This approach informs the character of each project to provide a unique response from a consistent architectural language. In the Lee house this is realized by a continuous flow of naturally lit, informal spaces linked by a clear, robust construction.

The Douglas Stephen Partnership
140-142 St. John Street
London EC1V 4UB
Tel: 0171-336 7884
Fax: 0171-336 7841
E-mail: DSPL140@aol.com
Directors: Barnaby Millburn, Geraldine Walder, and Simon Colebrook

The Douglas Stephen Partnership was formed in 1993 in succession to the practice originally founded by the late Douglas Stephen. The practice carries out a wide variety of projects and specializes in residential work including over 20 loft projects for individual clients with differing backgrounds and requirements.

Kelly Hoppen Interiors
2 Alma Studios, 32 Stratford Road
Kensington
London WB 6QF
Tel: 0171 938 4151
Fax: 0171 938 1878
Email: aposter@kellyhoppen.co.uk

The award-winning Kelly Hoppen has been acknowledged as one of Britain's most sought-after interior designers. Her cool, clean, and distinctive style has won her commissions from around the world, from top residences to corporate spaces. Hoppen's timeless designs, which combine the best of Eastern contemplation with Western grandeur, are all about balance, peace, serenity, and rejuvenation.

MMM Architects
The Banking Hall
28 Maida Vale
London W9 1RS
Tel: 0207 286 9499
Fax: 0207 286 9599
E-mail: post@mmm.demon.co.uk

Mark Davison helped launch Manhattan Loft Corporation. As a founding team member, he was instrumental in helping the company become one of the most influential in the industry. As a founder of MMM Architects with partners Min Hitchcox and Matthew Ratsma, he has developed a cutting-edge professional practice with an exemplary body of work.

Malin Iovino Design
43 St. Saviours Wharf
Mill Street
London SE1 2BA
Tel: 0171 252 3542
Fax: 0171 252 3542
Mob: 0956 326122

Malin Iovino's design style is clean and practical and strives to be contemporary and classical. Her objective is to create spaces that are comfortable, organized, and serene. Iovino believes that given the hectic pace we are exposed to in our daily routine, the home should be a place that stimulates the process of unwinding. The client plays a pivotal role in directing the creative inspiration. It is from listening to what the clients would like to achieve that ideas are triggered that will eventually lead to a unique design. While maintaining a precise design language, Iovino believes that the approach must be flexible and adapt to clients' needs and changing times.

Mark Guard Ltd. Architects
161 Whitfield Street
London W1P 5RY
Tel: 0171 380 1199
Fax: 0171 387 5441
E-mail: mga@markguard.co.uk
Web site: www.markguard.co.uk

Mark Guard Ltd. Architects consists of a small team of architects specializing in the development of elegant, functional, and modernist design. According to the team at Mark Guard, it is only through the act of building that the art of architecture can be explored and understood. The practice has had considerable success motivating contractors and fabricators to achieve technical advances within the industry and has led the way in the practical application of the theories of transformable space. Having achieved the desired function, emphasis is placed on space, light, and form. Drawing inspiration from the work of the early Modern Movement, the practice believes that good design should do more than merely resolve the brief; it should inspire and enhance the spirit.

Matthew Priestman Architects
6–8 Emerald Street
London WC1N 3QA
Tel: 0171 404 3113
Fax: 0171 404 1661
E-mail: mpa@mparch.demon.co.uk

Included in the Architecture Foundation's directory of New British Architects and recently at the Royal Institute of British Architects exhibition "Architecture on the Horizon," this internationally recognized architectural and urban-design practice is involved in a wide range of projects from strategic master planning, urban design, cultural facilities, higher education, and highly detailed interiors. Benefiting from the excellent human and technical resources of central London, the practice is fully equipped with CAD facilities and develops design proposals and production information with two-dimensional drawings and three-dimensional imaging. Physical models made in-house are also used extensively to express ideas and test spatial assumptions.

Michael Reeves Interior Design
33 Mossop Street
London SW3 2NB
Tel: 0171 225 2501
Fax: 0171 225 3060

Reeves opened his first shop in Chelsea in 1996, selling an eclectic mix of ethnic, oriental, antique, and contemporary furniture and accessories—a total change of career after more than twenty years as a fashion designer. In December 1998, he won the coveted Andrew Martin International Interior Designer of the Year award. The next February saw the launch of Reeves' own furniture line and a second store in Brompton Cross to accommodate the contemporary furniture with its supporting mix of accessories.

Moutarde
Flat 8, 8-13 New Inn Street
London ECZ A 3PY
Tel: 0171 684 8789

Moutarde is a young, small design-and-build company that loves developing the use of new materials and practicing innovative ideas while still being functional. They cover all areas of design: retail, residential, commercial, and restaurants and nightclubs. They believe that everyone should live and work in a well-designed environment, and that by passing on their experience to clients, it may help clients to appreciate good and bad design. Good design helps you to look at the world more closely and carefully.

Patel Taylor Architects
85 Royal College Street
London NW1 0SE
Tel: 0171 388 3223
Fax: 0171 388 3257
E-mail: pta@pateltaylor.demon.co.uk

Andrew Taylor and Pankaj Patel gained an early reputation following their success on a number of international competitions. Their collaboration led to the establishment of the practice in 1989. The client is seen as an integral part of their teamwork approach and whenever possible, Patel Taylor likes to develop the building and the design with clients using models, drawings, and CAD facilities, to explore, develop, and explain the projects. Their work encompasses a broad range of building types from sensitive conversions, studios, public buildings, highly crafted private homes, to large environmental projects such as the Thames Barrier Park.

Peter Wadley Architects
The Coach House
8 Avenue Crescent
London W3 8EW

Peter Wadley believes that interior architecture is as much about the relationship that will be formed by his clients with their living space as it is to do with the relationship between rooms, surfaces, and textures. Wadley's designs evolve through the careful understanding of the client, the function required from the building, and his own ability to enjoy design problems as they arise. It is an evolving process and the enthusiastic involvement of his clients, both intellectually and emotionally, feed, and feed off, his imagination. Peter's aims are to develop an architecture that feels physically good, that makes relevant, if sometimes surprising, connections between the user and the greater world beyond.

Powell-Tuck Associates
14 Barley Mow Passage
London W4 4PH
Tel: 0181 747 9988
Fax: 0181 747 8838
E-mail: jpowelltuck@powelltuck.co.uk

Powell-Tuck Associates' philosophy can be applied equally to new building work as it can to refurbishment. They provide contemporary solutions for contemporary society, ever mindful of the cultural importance of existing built form.

Reed Creative Services Limited
151a Sydney Street
London SW3 6NT
Tel: 0171 565 0066
Fax: 0171 565 0067

Reed Creative is an Interior Design practice specializing in highly detailed modern, residential work that covers all aspects of interior architecture and furniture. They use mainly craftsman-based finishing techniques, often developing new materials and textures in the course of their projects. The firm works internationally and believes strongly that their design must relate to the location of the project to be successful. Reed also has a furniture showroom in Sydney Street, London where their own designed furnishings are sold alongside antiques and decorative objects.

Rick Mather Architects
123 Camden High Street
London NW1 7JR
Tel: 0171 284 1727
Fax: 0171 267 7826
E-mail: rma@rmather.demon.co.uk

Rick Mather Architects' work spans both new-build renovation with especial interest in master planning combined with a renowned and innovative expertise in the intelligent reuse of existing structures, sustainable low-energy buildings, and advanced techniques in the use of glass. Recently completed projects include the new E20m Neptune Hall at the National Maritime Museum in Greenwich, the ISMA banking school at the University of Reading, and the 1998 RIBA National Award-winning private house in Hampstead. The most recent competition won is the master plan for London's South Bank Center, which includes the Royal Festival Hall, Queen Elizabeth Hall, Purcell Room, Hayward Gallery, National Film Theater, MOMI, and Jubilee Gardens.

Roland Cowan Architects
99 Westbourne Park Villas
London W2 5ED
Tel: 020 7229 5599
Fax: 020 7229 5566
E-mail: rdicowan@aol.com

Roland Cowan oversees all aspects of refurbishment and new construction from briefing and project appraisal to the detailed design of final finishes. Clients are encouraged to write about how they have lived in their previous homes—listing pros and cons. The firm maximizes the structural possibilities at the outset of a project. Storage planning is an integral part of the design. Residential projects mostly involve a total service, including furnishing, garden design, joinery design in unusual materials, and feature lighting, among other services.

Ruffle & Hook Interior
122-124 St. John Street
Clerkenwell, London EC1V 4JS
Tel: 0171 490 4321
Fax: 0171 490 1646

Carol Thomas at Ruffle & Hook has become synonymous with unusual colors and textures that aren't seen anywhere else. A rebel in design, Thomas is well-known for her wonderful contradictions, putting together old and new, French and English, linen and suede—textures and looks that clash in order to create her unusual and dramatic style. Thomas is especially regarded for her innovative curtain designs, trimming them with glass beads or fur, suede drapes or tailored linen blinds.

Simon Conder Associates
Nile Street Studios
8 Nile Street, London N17RF
Tel: 0171 251 2144
Fax: 0171 251 2145

Simon Conder Associates is a team of architects, interior designers, and furniture designers. This multidisciplinary expertise is applied analytically to all projects to develop creative, cost-effective solutions within tight financial and time constraints. Early on, the practice was dominated by conversion projects. Since 1986, the range and scale of the practice's work has grown considerably and now includes new-build projects on urban and rural sites, interior design for projects that vary in size and scale, and exhibition and retail design. Since 1988, the practice has also been working outside the U.K. with completed projects in Germany, Japan, and the U.S.

Stanton Williams
Diespeker Wharf
38 Graham Street
London N1 8JX
Tel: 0171 880 6400
Fax: 0171 880 6401

Stanton Williams is dedicated to the idea of architectural quality and responding to the unique demands of each project. Since its inception, the partnership has gained a strong reputation for its work on notable and prestigious projects. Together with a regular team of consultants it has produced a wide range of architectural projects from museums, galleries, theater, educational, retail and domestic work through to large commercial offices. Stanton Williams has a reputation for the quality of its design work and the ability to achieve creative contemporary design solutions within sensitive and important contexts.

Thomas de Cruz Architects Designers Ltd
80/82 Chiswick High Road
London W4 1SY
Tel: 020 8995 8100
Fax: 020 8995 8133

A progressive, London-based practice producing sensitive contemporary architecture with an emphasis on imaginative interiors and creative lighting, Thomas de Cruz Architects covers a wide variety of building types, including high-quality domestic designs for private clients. The firm often draws on the Mediterranean response to climate for inspiration, connecting the building to its surroundings with folding doors, canopies, and decks, creating serene spaces flooded with natural light. In the city, older properties with dark, cellular layouts are also liberated by this approach.

Timney Fowler Showroom
388 King's Road
London SW3 5UZ
Tel: 0171 352 2263
Fax: 0171 352 0351

A design and distribution company based in London with a showroom in Chelsea, offices in New York, and worldwide representation, the company was founded in 1979 by Susan Timney and Grahame Fowler, who began working together after graduating from the Royal College of Art. Timney Fowler has produced seven collections of interior furnishing fabrics and two collections of wallpapers, borders, and friezes. They also design for interiors and fashion.

Wells Mackereth Architects
Unit 14 Archer Street Studios
10-11 Archer Street
London WIV 7HG
Tel: 0171 287 5504
Fax: 0171 287 5506

The architects at Wells Mackereth see buildings as living organisms and they set out to design fluid, ambiguous places that fluctuate in mood, changeable settings generated for and by the people that use them. Their design work is characterized by a consistent attention to junctions and details, to express planes and volumes. They like to combine unexpected materials, intense colors, texture and light to create abstract settings and intriguing spaces for a modern way of life.

Will White Design
326 Portobello Road
London W10 6RU
Tel: 0181 964 8052
Fax: 0181 964 8050

Specializing in architectural and interior projects primarily for private individual clients who understand the value of carefully considered design, Will White's main areas include residential, offices, art galleries—from extending and redefining the space, to specific furniture design. Close relationships with clients create a continual conversation in which the design evolves with the client's own creative input.

ABOUT THE AUTHOR

Stafford Cliff's first ventures into the world of interior design was when, as a young designer working for Terence Conran's multi-disciplinary design company in London, he was given the job of designing and art-directing the Habitat Catalogue in 1972. A few years earlier, the shops had transformed the domestic furniture and housewares market with the opening of a chain of Habitat Shops that quickly spread throughout the UK. The twice-yearly mail-order catalogues went even further–photographing the products on location in real houses in England and France and later in New York, when the first Conran's opened in the USA. They quickly became collector's items and a set is held in the V&A Museum.

In 1974, he designed *The Housebook* for Conran–an innovative publication that was to become one of the best-selling home design manuals of all time, soon followed by *The Kitchen Book* and *The Bed and Bath Book.*

As creative director of Conran Design Group, he was responsible for designing and overseeing a vast range of projects, from corporate identities and packaging; to magazines, catalogues, and annual reports; to shopping centers and airports.

As co-author and designer, he created *French Style* with Suzanne Sleisin and photographer Jaques Dirand–a high quality survey of French interior design and lifestyles, that set the style and format for a new series of country-by-country books that combined–for the first time–travel, culture, history, and interiors–and, with eight subsequent titles, including Japan and the Caribbean, spawned a whole new publishing trend.

As an independent design consultant based in London, Cliff has continued to design and art-direct magazines and catalogues, and as an author, his books include–for Rockport–a series on various aspects of design, including restaurant graphics, specialty packaging, exhibition design, point-of-style, cutting edge typography, and catalogue design. He has produced two books that examine the history of design for the home from 1600 to 1930, in England and in France-shown through the design archives in factories and museums (*The English Archive* 1998, and *The French Archive* 1999). Most recently, he has also begun a new series of books about the process of design, *Trade Secrets of Great Design: Packaging*, and is currently working on a total of seven new books on design and the home.

PHOTO CREDITS

Peter Aprahamian, 144-149, 156-161, 182, 183, 186-187

Michael Lewis Bale, 168-173

Henry Bourne, 126-131

Richard Bryant/Arcaid, 10-13

Nick Carter of Southampton, Courtesy of IDH Ltd., 162-167

Keith Collie, 178-171

Thomas De Cruz, 100-103

Derek Wylie Architects, 104-109

Andreas von Einsiedel, 58-59, 61, 63, 138-143

Chris Gascoigne, 26-31, 48-51, 74-77, 86-91, 120-125

Dennis Gilbert, 116-119

© Richard Glover, 174-177, 184

Paul Harmer, 32-37

Ken Hayden, 92-99

Marcus Hilton Photography, 110-115

© Nicholas Kane, 78-81

James McMillan, 150-155

Eric Morin, 60, 62

© James Morris/Axiom, 38-43

Keith Parry Photography, 14-19

Ed Reeve, 52-57

Chris Tubbs, 82-85